Sew Fun & Easy
TABLE
FASHIONS™

Edited by Julie Johnson

HOUSE of
WHITE
BIRCHES

PUBLISHERS
SINCE 1947

Sew Fun & Easy Table Fashions™

EDITOR	Julie Johnson
ART DIRECTOR	Brad Snow
PUBLISHING SERVICES DIRECTOR	Brenda Gallmeyer
ASSOCIATE EDITOR	Kristine M. Frye
ASSISTANT ART DIRECTOR	Nick Pierce
COPY SUPERVISOR	Michelle Beck
COPY EDITORS	Nicki Lehman, Mary O'Donnell
TECHNICAL EDITOR	Marla Freeman
GRAPHIC ARTS SUPERVISOR	Ronda Bechinski
GRAPHIC ARTISTS	Glenda Chamberlain, Edith Teegarden
PRODUCTION ASSISTANTS	Marj Morgan, Judy Neuenschwander
TECHNICAL ARTIST	Nicole Gage
PHOTOGRAPHY SUPERVISOR	Tammy Christian
PHOTOGRAPHY	Don Clark, Matthew Owen
PHOTO STYLISTS	Tammy M. Smith, Tammy Steiner
CHIEF EXECUTIVE OFFICER	David J. McKee
BOOK MARKETING DIRECTOR	Dwight Seward

Printed in China
First Printing: 2008
Library of Congress Control Number: 2007933456
Hardcover ISBN: 978-1-59217-200-9
Softcover ISBN: 978-1-59217-204-7

DRGbooks.com

1 2 3 4 5 6 7 8 9

Welcome!

Combining your love of sewing with a love of fine dining to create fashionable table wear is what *Sew Fun & Easy Table Fashions* is all about.

We know that fine dining is a celebration of life, love and good friends. Whether you choose to dine inside or outside, plan a gala celebration or an intimate gathering for a few close friends, it's always fun to enhance your dining experience with the perfect table wear.

Perfect table wear helps you express your unique personality and will give family and friends a hint of what is to come. Combined with the wonderful aromas wafting from your kitchen, a well-dressed table will entice your guests and have them oohing and ahhing long before the main course is served.

"Perfect table wear helps you to express your unique personality."

I know you'll love the beautiful table fashions created by the talented group of designers that are featured in this book. They have really uncovered what it takes to cover a table, so much so, that you'll be able to create a fashionable, fabric-covered table for any occasion, any mood and in any style.

And like any fashion-conscious individual, having the perfect tabletop fashion is not enough. What is enough, is to dress your table with to-die-for table accessories: pretty bowls, baskets, bun warmers and more. After the fine dining is over, we've added some creative solutions for storage, so your table wear will always look its best.

We hope you have fun with this book, and that your dining is pleasurable.

Sew let's get started!

Julie

Contents

Table Wear
for Every Season

Remember when your Sunday best was just
for special occasions? After you sew a few
of these designs, you'll be so delighted with
your Sunday-best table fashion that you'll
always want your table to strut its stuff.

Organza Table Runner & Chair Topper

Designs by Carol Zentgraf

Impress friends and family with this elegant table setting. Don't ever tell them how easy it is to create—simply fuse purchased napkins together and add embellishments. Sew fun, sew easy, so beautiful!

Table Runner

Finished size
60 x 20 inches, including fringe

Materials
- 20 x 20-inch organza napkins:
    - 1 red
    - 2 gold
- 2½ yards ½-inch-wide gold gimp trim
- 1¼ yards gold tassel trim
- Acrylic crystal shapes:
    - 32 (21mm) ruby lilies
    - 32 (21mm) cognac lilies
    - 44 (10mm) ruby multifaceted squares
    - 44 (10mm) cognac multifaceted squares
- Gem adhesive
- Permanent fabric adhesive
- Fusible web tape
- Basic sewing supplies and equipment

Instructions

1. Apply fusible web tape to two opposite hemmed edges of the red organza napkin on the wrong side.

2. Remove paper backing and fuse each edge to the edge of a gold napkin (Figure 1).

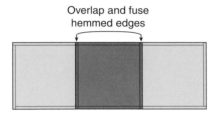

Overlap and fuse
hemmed edges

Figure 1

3. Cut four 21-inch lengths of gold gimp trim. Center a length on each fused edge, wrapping ends to the back and stitching in place with a zig-zag stitch. Use fabric adhesive to glue remaining lengths across runner 5½ inches from each end. Turn ends under and glue.

4. Cut length of tassel trim in half. Glue one length to each end of runner, wrapping trim ends to the back.

5. Referring to Figure 2, use a chalk pencil to draw four 5-inch squares across each space at the ends of the runner. Measure diagonally across each square and mark the center.

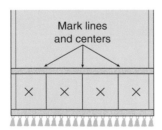

Mark lines
and centers

Figure 2

6. Using gem adhesive, glue eight acrylic squares evenly spaced on each side of each square, alternating colors. Glue an acrylic square in the center of each square, alternating colors. Glue four ruby acrylic lilies around each cognac square and four cognac lilies around each ruby square. Glue a lily

in each corner of each square, matching the color of the center square.

Chair Topper

Finished size
8¾ x 14½ inches

Materials
• 20 x 20-inch organza napkins:
    2 red
    1 gold
• 1¼ yards ½-inch-wide gold gimp trim
• 3½-inch-long gold tassel with hanging loop
• Acrylic crystal shapes:
    1 (21mm) ruby lily
    1 (10mm) ruby multifaceted square
• Gem adhesive
• Permanent fabric adhesive
• Fusible web:
    ¼-inch-wide tape
    8½ x 11-inch sheet
• Basic sewing supplies and equipment

Instructions

1. Apply fusible web tape to two adjacent edges of the gold organza napkin on the wrong side. Press the napkin in half diagonally, adhering remaining two edges to fused edges, leaving small opening at corner point unfused. Insert tassel loop into corner opening and fuse in place (Figure 3). Topstitch fused edges using red thread.

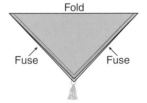

Fold

Fuse   Fuse

Figure 3

2. Sandwich the gold napkin between the right sides of both red napkins, aligning the fold of the gold napkin with the top edges of the red napkins. Sew sides and top together, stitching just inside napkin hems. Trim corners, turn right side out and press.

3. Trim 4½ inches from lower edges of red napkins, setting excess red organza aside for appliqué. Press under cut edge ½ inch and topstitch in place. Glue gimp trim around bottom edge.

4. Using template below, trace the word "JOY" onto paper backing of fusible web sheet; fuse to trimmed organza. Cut out letters and fuse to gold napkin 4 inches above the point.

5. Use gem adhesive to adhere acrylic crystal lily and square to point of gold napkin. 🌱

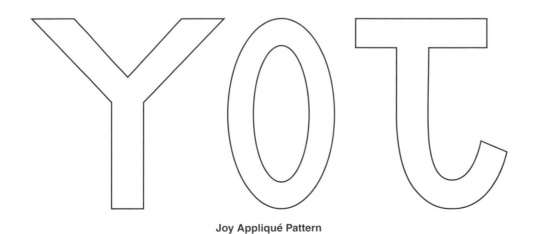

Joy Appliqué Pattern

Shadow-Stitched Table Runner

Design provided by Husqvarna Viking Sewing Machine Co.

Decorative serger stitching and sheer fabric are the perfect combination for a special table runner. Create a beautiful setting for a bridal or anniversary event!

Finished size
Adjustable to fit any size table (pictured runner is 10 x 56 inches)

Materials
- Organza fabric (yardage needed to match length of table plus 20 inches)
- 3 cones serger thread to match fabric
- 1 cone pearl rayon thread
- 2 decorative ribbon bows
- Water or air-soluble fabric pen
- Spray starch or sizing
- 4- or 5-thread serger with cover stitch feature
- Basic sewing supplies and equipment

Cutting
- Cut two pieces organza fabric each 21 inches wide x length of table plus 20 inches. Apply starch or sizing to each piece and press to add temporary firmness to fabric.

Shadow Stitching
1. Fold one selvage edge of one organza piece up to cut edge to create a 45-degree angle along fold

(Figure 1). Finger-press fold to make a crease in the fabric. Unfold fabric piece.

Figure 1

2. Using fabric pen and beginning at crease, draw diagonal lines 2½ inches apart along the entire length of the fabric piece (Figure 2).

Figure 2

3. With right sides up, place marked fabric piece over unmarked fabric piece. Hand- or machine-baste layers together between the marked lines and around the outer edges to reduce movement of fabric during next step.

4. Set serger for cover stitch. Thread both needles with serger thread. Thread pearl rayon thread in cover stitch looper.

5. With right side of fabric facing up, stitch along each marked diagonal line. Remove basting threads.

Assembly

1. Set serger for 3-thread overlock stitch. Thread loopers and needle with serger thread.

2. Fold fabric piece in half lengthwise with right sides together. Serge across long raw edges. Turn right side out. Press.

3. Hand- or machine-baste across each end of runner. Pull basting thread to gather ends tightly. Secure ends of gathering threads.

4. Fold gathered edges under and tack in place on wrong side of runner. Attach a decorative ribbon bow to each end. 🍴

Strawberry Dream

Cool and light, but not too sweet, this dessert is sure to please.

> **2 pasteurized egg whites**
> **1 tablespoon sugar**
> **1 cup fat-free, light vanilla yogurt**
> **1 tablespoon orange juice concentrate, thawed**
> **5 cups frozen strawberries, thawed and well-drained, divided**

Beat the egg whites until stiff peaks form. Gradually beat in sugar. Fold in the yogurt and thawed juice concentrate. In separate bowl, mash one cup of berries. Fold into egg white mixture. Alternate remaining strawberries with egg white mixture in parfait glasses, reserving enough berries to cover the top. Serve immediately. Serves 4.

Sweet on You

Design by Carolyn Vagts

Pink, purple and passion are the inspiration behind this sweet Valentine's Day concoction of batik and traditional quilting fabric. Low calorie, but oh so sweet, you'll capture someone's heart with this creation.

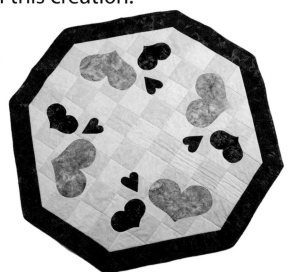

Finished size
32¾ x 32¾ inches

Materials
- 45-inch-wide fabric:
  - ½ yard light pink for center squares
  - ½ yard medium pink for center squares
  - ⅔ yard fuchsia for border and binding
- 1 yard coordinating fabric for backing
- Scraps 3 coordinating batik fabrics for heart appliqués
- 1 yard batting
- 1 yard fusible web
- Basic sewing supplies and equipment

Cutting
From light pink fabric for squares:
• Cut four 3½-inch strips the width of the fabric; subcut strips into 40 (3½-inch) squares.

From medium pink fabric for squares:
• Cut four 3½-inch strips the width of the fabric; subcut strips into 41 (3½-inch) squares.

From fuchsia fabric for border and binding:
• Cut four 2-inch strips the width of the fabric for binding.
• Cut four 2½-inch strips the width of the fabric; subcut strips into four 2½ x 14-inch rectangles and four 2½ x 18-inch rectangles for border.

From scraps of batik fabric for appliqué:
• Apply fusible web to fabric. Using patterns provided (page 17), cut four each large, medium and small hearts.

Assembly

Use ¼-inch-wide seam allowances unless otherwise stated.

1. Sew one 3½-inch light pink square to both ends of a 3½-inch medium pink square (Figure 1). Make 13 units.

Figure 1

2. Sew one 3½-inch medium pink square to both ends of a light pink square (Figure 2). Make 14 units.

Figure 2

3. Using the units from steps 1 and 2, make a total of nine blocks a shown in Figures 3A and 3B: four blocks with light pink corners and five blocks with medium pink corners.

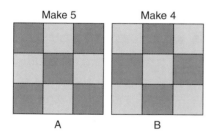

Figure 3

4. Referring to Figure 4 for placement, sew blocks together to make a large square.

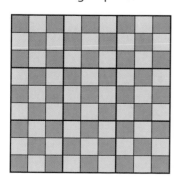

Figure 4

5. At each corner block, measure ¼ inch from seams at points indicated in Figure 5. Draw a line across each corner block and cut away the corner on this line to make center piece.

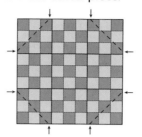

Figure 5

6. Sew a 2½ x 14-inch border rectangle to each trimmed corner, leaving extra at ends for trimming (Figure 6).

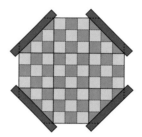

Figure 6

7. Trim borders as shown in Figure 7, following the edges of the center section.

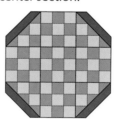

Figure 7

8. Sew on 2½ x 18-inch rectangles to the remaining four sides; trim to size using the outer edges of the border as a guide (Figure 8).

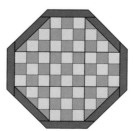

Figure 8

Fusible Tips

When tracing appliqué shapes on the paper side of fusible web, be sure to allow enough space between shapes so each can be cut loosely around the tracing lines.

Always test the heat time. Different irons heat at different rates.

An appliqué sheet is great for assembling pieces that are layered prior to final placement. It ensures fewer mistakes.

Cut out traced pieces approximately ¼ inch from traced lines; iron onto the wrong side of the fabric and cut on the traced lines. ***Note:*** *There is no wrong side on high-quality batik fabrics.*

Always start fusing with the pieces in the background first, working to the ones in the foreground. Layering gives dimension and helps with shading.

9. Position and fuse appliqués in place referring to photo for placement.

10. Cut backing to fit runner. Sandwich batting between runner and backing. Stitch around edges of appliqué and stitch-in-the-ditch to quilt.

11. Using ⅝-inch seam allowance (and trimming seam to ⅜ inch), bind edges of runner with 2-inch-wide strips. 🍽

Nutty Stuffed Mushrooms

There are never any left over!

**10 large fresh mushrooms
1 small onion, chopped
3 tablespoons butter
¼ cup dry bread crumbs
¼ cup finely chopped pecans
3 tablespoons Parmesan cheese
¼ teaspoon salt
¼ teaspoon dried basil
Dash cayenne pepper**

Preheat oven to 400 degrees. Remove mushroom stems and chop. Brown onion and chopped stems in butter for approximately 5 minutes; set aside. In bowl, combine bread crumbs, pecans, cheese, salt, basil and pepper. Add mushroom stems and onion. Stuff into mushroom caps. Place on greased baking dish. Bake uncovered 15 to 18 minutes. Makes 10.

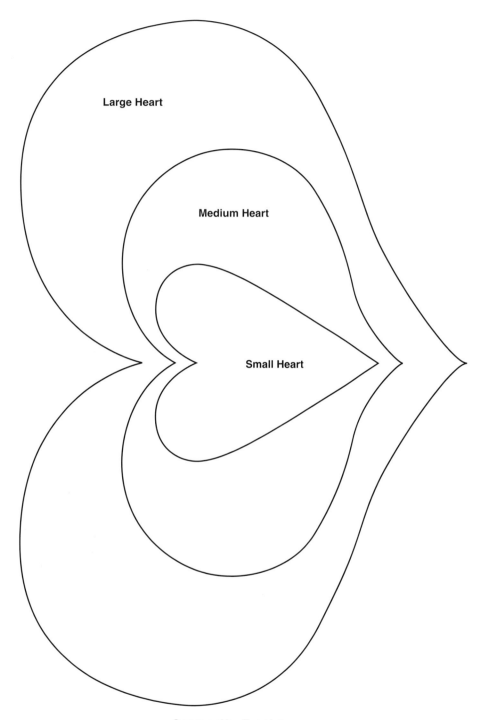

Large Heart

Medium Heart

Small Heart

Sweet on You Templates

Love Is in the Stars!

Designs by Michele Crawford for Coats & Clark

Combine easy appliqué and piecing with cheery prints to create this lighthearted table setting. It's perfect for a valentine luncheon—or just because.

Finished sizes
Place Mat: 12½ x 18½ inches
Napkin: 19 x 19 inches
Table Runner: 12½ x 42½ inches

Materials
• 44/45-inch-wide cotton fabrics:
  ⅓ yard pink/blue plaid for star points
  ⅝ yard white tone-on-tone print for block centers, edges and corners
  ⅝ yard blue floral print for sashing and borders
  1⅜ yards pink print for napkins, heart appliqués and binding
  1⅜ yards multicolored plaid or bold check for place mat borders, place mat backing and runner backing
• 1 yard low-loft batting
• ¼ yard paper-backed fusible web
• Coats & Clark Color Twist thread: bashful pink
• Basic sewing supplies and equipment

Note: *Yardage and instructions are for a runner, two place mats and two napkins. Preshrink fabrics before cutting. Usable fabric width should be 40 inches after washing.*

Cutting
From white tone-on-tone print for block background:
• Cut six 4½-inch squares for the block centers.
• Cut three 2½ x 40-inch strips; subcut strips into 24 (2½ x 4½-inch) rectangles for block edges.
• Cut two 2½ x 40-inch strips; subcut strips into 24 (2½-inch) squares for corners.

From pink/blue plaid for star points:
• Cut three 2½ x 40-inch strips; subcut strips into 48 (2½-inch) squares.

From the blue floral print for sashing and borders:
• Cut seven 2½ x 40-inch strips. Set aside three of these strips for runner sashing and borders.
• From the remaining strips, cut nine 2½ x 8½-inch strips and four 2½ x 12½-inch strips.

From pink print for napkins, binding and heart appliqués:
• Cut two 24-inch squares for the napkins.
• Cut six 2¼ x 40-inch strips for binding strips.
• Cut one 4½ x 40-inch strip. Apply fusible web. Using pattern provided (page 21), cut out six heart appliqués.

From multicolored plaid or bold check for runner backing, place mat backing and place mat borders:
• Cut one 13 x 43-inch strip from the length of the fabric for the runner backing.
• Cut two 13 x 19-inch pieces for place mat backing.
• Cut four 3½ x 12½-inch strips for place mat borders.

From batting:
• Cut two 13 x 19-inch pieces for place mats.
• Cut one 13 x 43-inch strip for runner.

Block Assembly

Use ¼-inch-wide seam allowances throughout.

1. With right sides together and raw edges aligned, stitch a 2½-inch pink/blue plaid square to each end of each 2½ x 4½-inch white rectangle (Figure 1). Trim away the corner ¼ inch from the stitching. Press the triangle toward the seam allowance to make 24 star-point units.

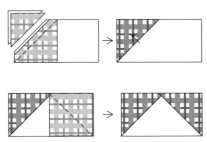

Figure 1

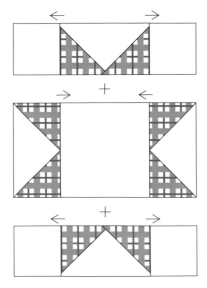

Figure 2

2. Sew two star-point units to opposite sides of a center block. Sew a white corner block to each end of two star-point units (Figure 2). Press seams in direction of arrows. Sew units together to make a block. Repeat to make six blocks.

Place Mat & Napkin Assembly

1. Sew a 2½ x 8½-inch blue floral print sashing strip to the top and bottom of one block. Press the seams toward the strips.

2. Arrange two 2½ x 12½-inch blue floral sashing strips and two 3½ x 12½-inch place mat multi-colored border strips as shown in Figure 3. Sew together for place mat top. Press all seams away from the center blocks. Repeat steps 1 and 2 for second place mat.

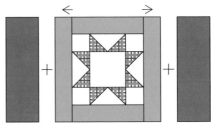

Figure 3

3. For each place mat, pin batting between the wrong sides of a 13 x 19-inch backing piece and a pieced place mat top. Use white machine-quilting thread to stitch in the ditch around the outer edges of each center square. Stitch in the ditch of the vertical border seams. Stitch the layers together ⅛ inch from the outer edge of the place mat; trim the batting and backing even with the pieced place mat edges.

4. Using bias seams, sew the 2¼-inch-wide pink print binding strips together to make one long strip; press the seams open (Figure 4). Fold the strip in half lengthwise with wrong sides together and press. Bind edges of each place mat with the bias strip, mitering corners and overlapping ends to finish. **Note:** *Remaining bias strip will be used on the runner.*

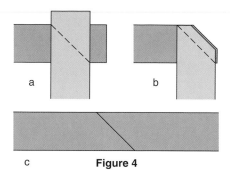

c   **Figure 4**

5. Remove the paper backing from two heart appliqués. Position and fuse a heart in the center of the star block on each place mat. Using the bashful pink thread, appliqué (blanket stitch or pin stitch) around the outer edge of each heart.

6. Turn under, press and sew a narrow double hem on each napkin square.

Runner Assembly

Note: *Refer to Figure 5 for Steps 1, 2 and 4.*

1. Sew remaining four blocks and five 2½ x 8½-inch blue floral print sashing strips together for runner. Press all seams toward blue strips.

2. Sew the three remaining 2½ x 40-inch blue floral print strips together using bias seams. Press the seams open. From the strip, cut two 2½ x 42½-inch border strips. Sew these strips to opposite edges of the panel to complete the pieced runner top.

3. Pin runner batting between 13 x 43-inch runner backing and pieced runner top. Stitch in the ditch around the outer edges of each center square. Stitch in the ditch of the vertical border seams. Stipple-quilt the sashing and border strips with blue machine-quilting thread. Stitch ⅛ inch from the outer edges of the pieced runner. Trim batting and backing even with the edges of top.

4. Remove the paper backing from four heart appliqués. Position and fuse a heart in the center of each star block on runner. Using the bashful pink thread, appliqué (blanket stitch or pin stitch) around the outer edge of each heart. ✿

Figure 5

**Love Is in the Stars
Appliqué Template**
Actual Size

Go Fly a Kite!

Designs by Pam Lindquist for Coats & Clark

Quilted swirls in the background of these colorful place mats hint at a breezy spring day filled with soaring kites. Colorful ribbon tails embellish the matching napkin wraps.

Finished sizes
Place Mat: 14½ x 18½ inches
Napkin Wrap: 4 x 7 inches, excluding kite tails
Napkin: 18¾ x 18¾ inches

Materials
• 44/45-inch-wide cotton quilting fabric:
    1⅛ yards blue tone-on-tone print for place mat centers
    ¼ yard blue print for inner borders
    1⅝ yards green multicolored print for outer borders and backing
    1⅝ yards green tone-on-tone print for napkins and napkin wrap backs
• ½ yard total assorted bright print scraps for kites
• 1 yard muslin for place mat backing
• Quilt batting
• Paper-backed fusible web
• Template plastic
• Heavy-weight fusible interfacing
• 8 yards ¼- or ⅜-inch-wide multicolored ribbon for kite tails
• ⅝ yard ¼-inch-wide green grosgrain ribbon for napkin wrap loops
• Tear-away stabilizer
• Large-eye needle with sharp point
• Optional: walking foot for quilting
• Basic sewing supplies and equipment

Cutting
All measurements include a ¼-inch-wide seam allowance unless otherwise stated. Preshrink and press all fabrics before cutting. Yardages given are based on 42 inches of usable width after preshrinking. Cut all strips across the fabric width.

From the blue tone-on-tone print for place mat centers:
• Cut four 17 x 21-inch rectangles.

From the blue print for the inner borders:
• Cut seven ¾ x 42-inch strips; subcut strips into eight ¾ x 10½-inch strips and eight ¾ x 15-inch strips.

From the green multicolored print for outer borders and backing:
• Cut one 11 x 42-inch strip; subcut strip into eight 2½ x 11-inch strips.
• Cut four 2½ x 42-inch strips; subcut strips into eight 2½ x 19-inch strips.
• Cut four 15 x 19-inch rectangles.

From the green tone-on-tone print for napkins and napkin wrap backs:
• Cut two 5½ x 42-inch strips; subcut strips into eight 5½ x 9-inch rectangles for napkin wrap backs.
• Cut four 19-inch squares for napkins.

From the assorted bright print scraps for kites:
• Cut (16) 3 x 9-inch rectangles.

From muslin for place mat backing:
• Cut four 17 x 21-inch rectangles.

From quilt batting:
• Cut four 17 x 21-inch rectangles.

From paper-backed fusible web:
• Cut eight 5 x 8-inch rectangles.

From heavy-weight fusible interfacing:
• Cut eight 5 x 8-inch rectangles.

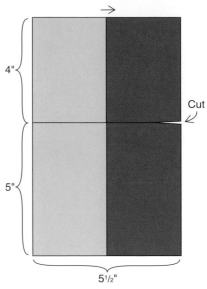

Figure 1

2. Arrange the pieces as shown in Figure 2 to create eight checkerboard rectangles. With right sides together and centers matching, stitch each set of rectangles together. Press the seam allowance open in the direction of arrow on each pair.

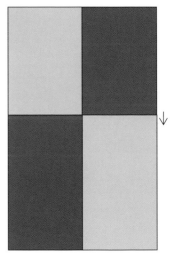

Figure 2

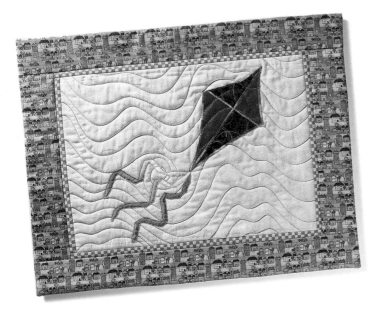

Place Mat Assembly

1. With right sides together, sew two 3 x 9-inch kite rectangles together along the long edge. Press the seam allowance toward the darker color in the pair. Repeat with the remaining rectangles. Cut each of the rectangle pairs into two pieces, one measuring 4 x 5½ inches and the other 5 x 5½ inches (Figure 1).

3. Set four pieced rectangles aside for the napkin wraps. Apply fusible web to the wrong side of the four remaining pieced rectangles.

4. Trace the template for the kite appliqué (page 27), including the cross lines, onto template plastic and cut out carefully. Position the template right side up on the right side of each of the four pieced rectangles with the cross lines aligned with the seam lines; cut out each kite (Figure 3).

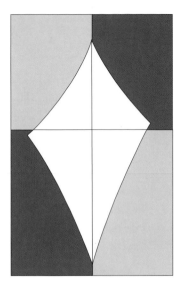

Figure 3

5. Position and fuse a kite on each place mat center panel, slightly off-center. Apply a piece of stabilizer on the wrong side of the panel behind each kite. Adjust the sewing machine for a narrow satin stitch and thread the needle with multicolored thread. Stitch over the outer edges and along the seam lines. Remove the stabilizer.

6. Sandwich batting rectangles between muslin place mat backing rectangles and place mat center panels. Pin or hand-baste the layers together. Draw a 10½ x 14½-inch rectangle around the kite, noting the positioning of the kite points (Figure 4). Thread machine with blue quilting thread and quilt as desired.

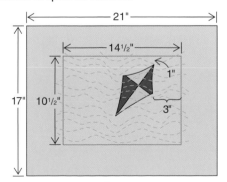

Figure 4

7. Cut the multicolored ribbon into 32 (8-inch) lengths. Set aside all but 12 lengths of ribbon.

Thread three ribbons into the large-eye needle and insert the needle at the point of the kite. Pull 1 inch of the ribbons to the wrong side and hand-tack the ends to the backing fabric. Arrange the ribbons on the surface to represent kite tails blowing in the wind (see photo). Machine-stitch each edge of each ribbon in place to within 1 inch of the end. Thread the ends through the needle, pull through to the back and tack in place.

8. With right sides together, pin a ¾ x 10½-inch blue print strip to one short edge of the drawn rectangle. Stitch ¼ inch from the raw edges and turn the strip against the place mat front; press. Add a strip to the opposite edge in the same manner, followed by the ¾ x 15-inch strips to the upper and lower edges (Figure 5).

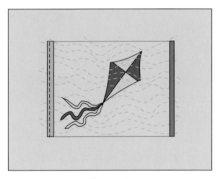

Figure 5

9. Pin, stitch, flip and press the 2½ x 11-inch border strips to each place mat as you did for the inner borders. Add the 2½ x 19-inch strips in the same manner.

10. With the kite facing up, trim the excess batting and backing even with the outer edges of the green borders (Figure 6).

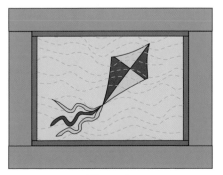

Figure 6

11. With right sides facing and using a ¼-inch-wide seam allowance, pin and sew a 15 x 19-inch green print rectangle to each place mat front, leaving a 5-inch opening for turning. Remove the pins, clip the corners and turn right side out. Press. Hand sew to finish.

12. Attach a walking foot or engage the even-feed feature if available on your machine. Stitch in the ditch of the border seam lines.

Napkin Wrap Assembly

1. Following the manufacturer's directions, apply a 5 x 8-inch piece of heavy-weight fusible interfacing to the wrong side of each of the four remaining pieced rectangles and to each of the 5½ x 9-inch green tone-on-tone rectangles. Apply a 5 x 8-inch piece of paper-backed fusible web to the interfacing on the wrong side of each green tone-on-tone rectangle. Remove the paper backing.

2. With interfacings together, place a pieced rectangle on top of a green tone-on-tone rectangle and pin the layers together in each corner.

3. Trace the kite template for the napkin on a piece of template plastic and cut out. Position it on each pieced rectangle with the crossbars matching the seam lines and cut out each double-layer kite (Figure 7).

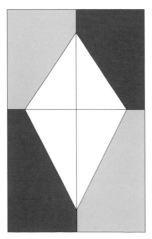

Figure 7

4. Arrange the remaining 8-inch lengths of ribbon in four groups of five ribbons each. Tuck the ribbon ends of one bunch between the two layers of each pair of kites and pin in place. Fuse the kite layers together, securing the kite tails.

5. Adjust the machine for a narrow satin stitch as for the place mats. Thread the needle with multicolored thread and satin-stitch over the raw edges and seam lines of each kite. Apply seam sealant to the cut ends of the ribbons.

6. Cut the ¼-inch-wide green grosgrain ribbon into four 4½-inch lengths. Turn under ¼ inch at each end of each ribbon and tack a ribbon to the back of each kite at the side points.

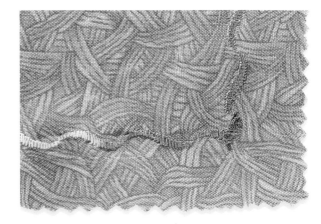

Napkin Finishing

1. Select a zigzag or decorative stitch on your machine and thread the machine with multicolored thread. With the right side of the fabric facing up, stitch ¾ inch from the raw edges of each napkin, pivoting at the corners.

2. Use pinking shears to trim away ⅛ inch along each raw edge to finish, or do a rolled-edge or double-narrow hem if you prefer. ❦

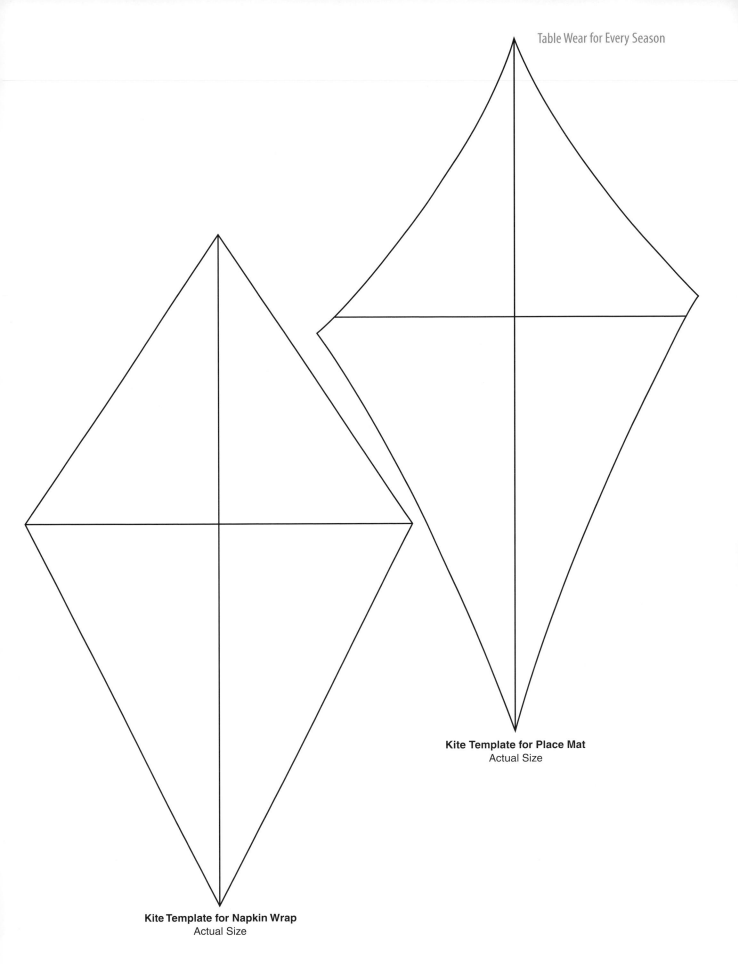

Kite Template for Place Mat
Actual Size

Kite Template for Napkin Wrap
Actual Size

Bunny in Style

Design by Carolyn S. Vagts

Be quick, like a bunny, and make this stylish bunny table topper for your spring celebration.

Finished size
38¼ x 15 inches

Materials
- ¼ yard 45-inch-wide white solid fabric for bunny face
- 1⅜ yards 45-inch-wide multicolored pastel fabric for background, outer border, backing and binding
- ⅛ yard 45-inch-wide yellow solid fabric for accent border
- 40 x 17-inch piece thin batting
- Fabric scraps for appliqué:
    white solid*
    pink batik
    light green batik
- Fusible web
- 4 (½-inch) black buttons
- Basic sewing supplies and equipment

Scraps of white solid fabric for bunny face were used on model project.

Cutting
From fabric for bunny face:
- Cut two 6½-inch squares.

From fabric for background, outer border, backing and binding:
- Cut one 10 x15-inch rectangle for center.
- Cut three 2½-inch strips the width of the fabric. Subcut strips into four 6 x 2½-inch and four 10 x 2½-inch rectangles.
- Cut eight 2-inch squares.
- Cut three 2½-inch strips the width of the fabric for border.
- Cut three 2-inch-wide strips the width of the fabric for binding.

***Note:** Backing will be cut later.*

From yellow solid fabric for accent border:
- Cut three 1¼-inch strips the width of the fabric.

From fabric scraps for appliqué:
- Apply fusible web to the backs of scrap fabrics. Using patterns provided (page 31), cut left and right ears, left and right inner ears, nose and bow to make two bunnies.

Assembly

Use ¼-inch-wide seam allowances unless otherwise stated.

1. On the wrong side of each 2-inch square, draw a diagonal line from corner to corner. Position four 2-inch squares on each white 6-inch square and stitch across diagonal lines (Figure 1). Make two units. Trim off outer triangles and press into a square.

Figure 1

2. Sew a 6 x 2½-inch rectangle to each end of a square unit from step 1; press. Sew the 10 x 2½-inch rectangles to the top and bottom of the same unit (Figure 2). Make two units.

Note: *Assembled unit should measure 10 x 10 inches.*

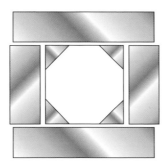

Figure 2

3. Sew a 10 x 10-inch unit to each 10-inch end of the 10 x 15-inch rectangle to make the center unit. Press.

4. Sew the 1¼-inch accent border to each long side of the center unit; trim ends. Sew accent border to each end and trim to size. Press.

5. Sew 2½-inch outer border strips in same manner as accent border (Figure 3). Press.

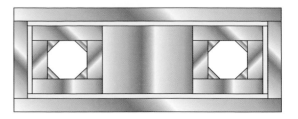

Figure 3

6. Using the photo as a reference, arrange appliqué pieces on runner and fuse in place. Cut backing from multicolored pastel to fit. Sandwich batting between runner and backing.

7. Stitch edges and detail of appliqué pieces, and stitch-in-the-ditch to quilt. Machine-embroider mouth with narrow satin stitch.

8. Using ⅝-inch seam allowance (and trimming seam to ⅜ inch), bind edges of runner with 2-inch-wide strips. Sew black buttons on for eyes. 🍴

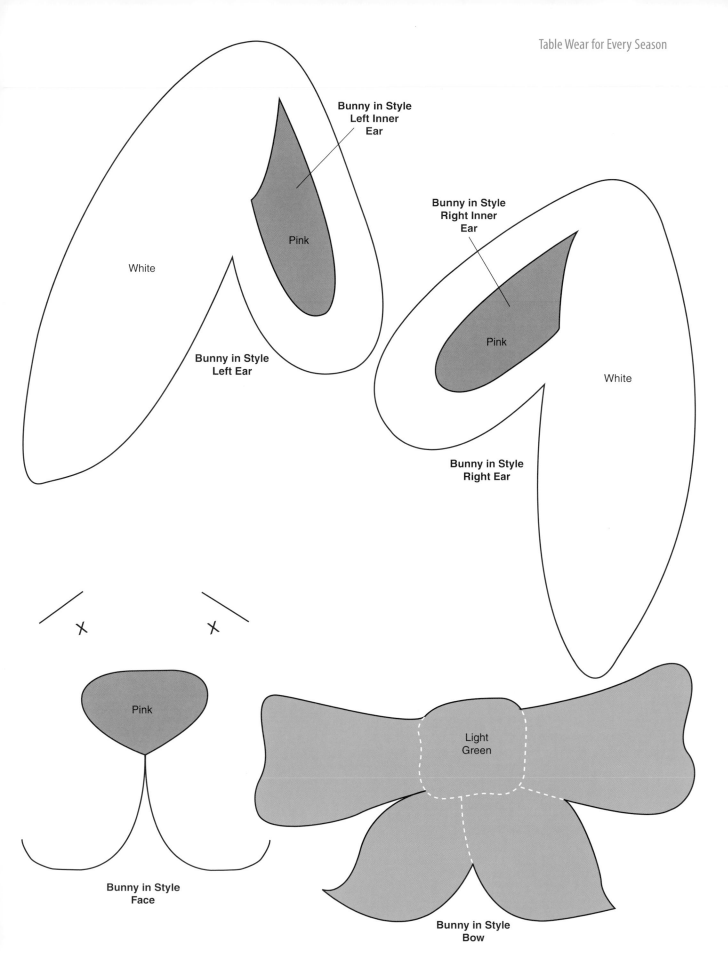

Bunny in Style
Left Inner
Ear

Pink

White

Bunny in Style
Left Ear

Bunny in Style
Right Inner
Ear

Pink

White

Bunny in Style
Right Ear

X   X

Pink

Light
Green

Bunny in Style
Face

Bunny in Style
Bow

Patriotic Party Set

Designs provided by Brother International Corporation

Perfect for a Memorial Day or Fourth of July party, these table accessories add a special touch to your holiday events. Easy piecing techniques help you stitch the quilt blocks quickly.

Finished sizes
Table Runner: 12½ x 60 inches
Place Mat: 11 x 16 inches
Napkin: 17½ x 17½ inches

Materials
• 45-inch-wide cotton fabrics:
>   2 yards blue star print
>   2½ yards white-on-white print
>   2 yards red print
• 4 (10 x 15-inch) pieces fusible interfacing
• Sewing thread to match fabrics
• Low-loft batting
• Optional: temporary spray adhesive
• Basic sewing supplies and equipment

Cutting
Note: *Fabric pieces for blocks will be cut from leftover white, red and blue fabrics, according to paper-piecing pattern.*

From red print:
• Cut four pieces each 10 x 15 inches for place mat backing.
• Cut four pieces each 18 x 18 inches for napkins.

From white-on-white print:
• Cut one piece 13 x 61 inches for table runner backing.
• Cut four pieces each 10 x 15 inches for place mat front.
• Cut four pieces each 18 x 18 inches for napkins.

From blue star print:
• Cut two pieces each 1½ x 61 inches and two pieces each 1½ x 14 inches for runner binding.
• Cut four strips each 1¼ x 72 inches for place mat borders.

Table Runner Assembly
Use ¼ inch for all seam allowances unless otherwise stated.

1. Make 20 copies of block pattern on page 34. Using paper-piecing instructions on page 35, make 20 blocks with fabrics.

2. For runner top, arrange blocks matching blue sections together (see photo) in two rows of ten blocks each. Stitch blocks together.

3. Layer top, batting and backing with right sides out. Baste layers together.

4. Using white thread, quilt as desired. Trim backing and batting to match front.

5. Stitch long binding pieces to each long edge of runner top. Press raw edges of runner binding under ¼ inch. Turn to back of runner and hand-sew edge of binding in place. Repeat with short binding pieces on short edges of runner.

Napkin Assembly

1. Stitch matching red and white fabric squares right sides together, leaving an opening for turning. Turn right side out. Press.

2. Fold raw edges of opening to inside and sew closed.

Place Mat Assembly

1. Stitch 1¼-inch border strips to long edges of front piece, right sides together. Repeat on short edges. Press.

2. Fold in each corner of front to form a 45-degree angle at fold. Press a crease in fabric at each fold (Figure 1). Trim off each corner ¼ inch from crease.

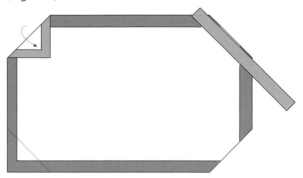

Figure 1

3. Extending cut end past edge slightly, stitch 1¼-inch border strip to one diagonal raw edge (Figure 1). Press seam allowance toward border. Cut ends of diagonal border to match outer edge of horizontal and vertical borders. Repeat at each corner.

4. Attach interfacing to wrong side of place mat back. Trim interfaced back piece to match shape of front. Stitch front and back, right sides together, leaving an opening at center of one long edge for turning. Trim seams at corners. Turn right side out. Press. Sew opening closed.

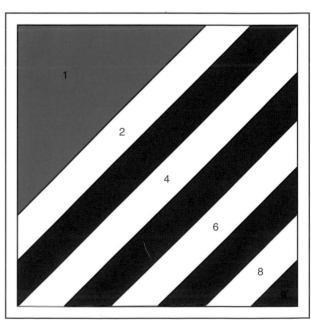

Patriotic Party Set
Flag block pattern
Enlarge 200%

Paper-Piecing Instructions

Each paper-piecing pattern is used just once. Make enough copies to match the number of blocks in the design.

Stitch the blocks together on the paper, following the printed lines; then tear the paper off and discard it.

The number sequence on the paper pattern shows the order in which to add the fabric pieces as you work.

The paper pattern keeps fabric from stretching as it is sewn. The finished size of each block will be the same.

Trim paper to ½ inch beyond the outer edge of the block pattern. Keep the paper block whole; do not cut out the pieces of the design.

During piecing, the fabric pieces need to be just large enough to completely cover the patch outline on the paper pattern, extending at least ¼ inch beyond the outline of the patch.

Cutting does not have to be exact, but allow enough for seam allowances. It is better to be too large than too small.

Before adding each new fabric piece to the paper pattern, make sure it is large enough to cover the patch outline on the pattern.

When joining the fabric pieces, set the machine to make small straight stitches (18–20 per inch). Begin and end the stitching ¼ inch from each end of the pattern line. Do not backstitch at the ends of the seam line.

When pressing, use a dry iron and press straight down. Finger pressing works well also.

Do not tear any of the pattern away until the block is complete.

To begin each block, position fabric piece No. 1 right side up on the unprinted side of the pattern in its correct location. If edges of fabric do not extend beyond the pattern, hold the layers up to a light and check to make sure the edges extend far enough past the outline. Adjust and pin, or glue fabric in place on the wrong side of the paper pattern.

Pin fabric piece No. 2 over fabric piece No. 1, right sides together. With printed side of pattern up, stitch along the seam line between the two patches; press. Turn fabric side up and press seam open.

Fold the paper pattern back on itself along the line you just stitched to expose the seam allowance; trim to ¼ inch.

Add each new fabric piece in the same manner as piece No. 2. When piecing is complete, trim outer edge of block ¼ inch from outer seam line on pattern.

Sewing Seashells by the Seashore

Designs by Janis Bullis

The out-of-the-ordinary circular place mat creatively frames your dish, and a seashell edge enhances the coordinating colors of solid linen fabric. Complete the ensemble with grosgrain-covered napkin rings and a decorative stitch to finish the napkins.

Finished size
Place Mat: 14 inches in diameter
Napkin: 18 inches square

Materials
• 2 colors mediumweight linen fabric:
⅝ yard darker fabric for border, backing and napkin*
½ yard lighter fabric for center*
• 15-inch square low-loft quilt batting
• 1½ yards ⅝-inch-wide grosgrain ribbon to match fabric
• 24 (1-inch) seashells
• 20 feet (or more) 28-gauge covered wire
• Wooden or plastic napkin ring
• Hot-glue gun
• High-speed rotary tool and drill bit
• Needle-nose pliers
• Basic sewing supplies and equipment

½ yard of each fabric is enough to make 3 place mats.

Cutting
From darker fabric:
• Cut one place mat border on fold, as shown on template on page 40.
• Cut one 15-inch-diameter place mat backing, as shown on template on page 40.
• Cut one piece ¼ inch larger than 18 inches square for napkin. Measure 18 inches following the threads of the crosswise and lengthwise grains. Pull threads exactly on the measurement and cut along pulled threads for a perfect 18-inch square (Figure 1 on page 38).

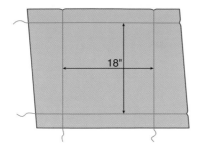

Figure 1

From lighter fabric:
• Cut one 11-inch-diameter place mat center.

From quilt batting:
• Cut one 15-inch-diameter using place mat backing template.

Place Mat Assembly
Use ½-inch-wide seam allowances throughout.

1. Staystitch a scant ½ inch from inner edge of border piece. Clip to stitching every ½ inch around.

2. Mark inner edge of border and outer edge of center into four equal quarters (Figure 2).

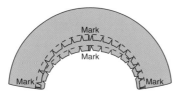

Figure 2

3. With right sides of fabric together and raw edges even, pin inner edge of border to outer edge of center, matching markings (Figure 3).

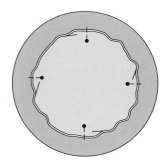

Figure 3

4. To make top of place mat, stitch border to center just outside ½-inch staystitching. Press seam open, and then press seam toward outer edge.

5. Baste quilt-batting circle to wrong side of place mat top, stitching ¼ inch from outer edge. Trim batting close to basting stitches to reduce bulk (Figure 4).

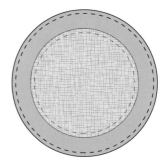

Figure 4

6. With right sides together, machine-stitch place mat top and place mat backing together ½ inch from outer edge, leaving a 4-inch opening for turning.

7. Turn place mat right side out. Hand-stitch opening closed and press place mat flat. Mark outer edge of place mat into 16 equal sections for placement of seashells.

8. Using the rotary tool and drill bit, drill a small hole in each seashell. Hand-stitch seashells around outer edge of place mat.

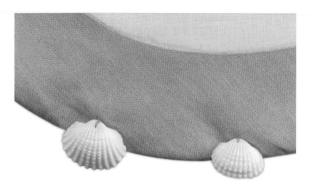

3. Glue one end of grosgrain ribbon to inside of napkin ring and begin wrapping ribbon around the ring, through the center. Every second pass, place a seashell over the last wrap made so wire extends onto unwrapped napkin ring. Apply a small dab of glue to wire and continue to wrap. Continue until napkin ring is covered with ribbon and shells make a complete circle around the outside. Trim excess ribbon and glue end to inside of ring. 🖈

Napkin Assembly

1. Measure 1 inch from each outside edge of napkin square. Pull one or two threads at this mark on each edge, distorting the weave (Figure 5).

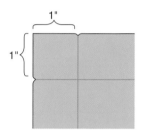

Figure 5

2. Using a zigzag or forward-moving decorative stitch, stitch along distorted line.

3. Pull threads on outer edges to create fringe of desired length.

Napkin Ring Assembly

1. Using rotary tool with drill bit, drill a small hole in seven or eight seashells. *Note: The number of seashells will depend on the size of the shell and the circumference of the napkin ring.*

2. Cut a 9-inch length of wire for each seashell. Use needle-nose pliers to bend one end of each length into a small knot. Insert opposite end of wire through hole in seashell so knot will be on the outside of the shell.

Tip

Choose a loosely woven linen, cotton or blend to simplify pulling threads from the fabric for fringing.

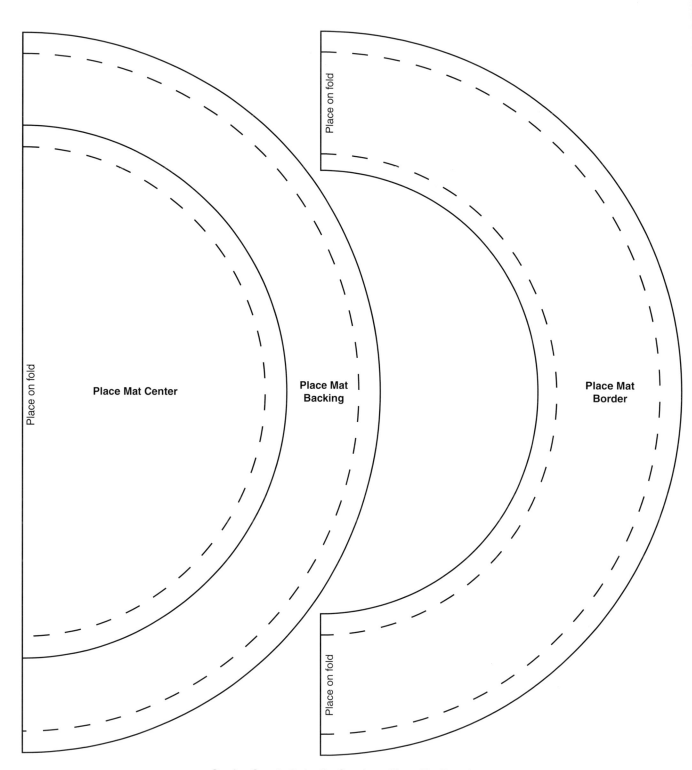

Sewing Seashells by the Seashore Place Mat Templates
Enlarge 200%

Falling Leaves Luncheon Set

Designs by Marta Alto

Colorful fall foliage frames the borders of this simply styled place mat. Create matching napkins to set the tone for fall feasting during the autumn holidays.

Finished sizes
Place Mat: 12 x 18 inches
Napkin: 18 x 18 inches

Materials for set of four
- 44/45-inch-wide cotton fabric:
    - ⅞ yard brown tone-on-tone print for borders
    - 2½ yards rust solid or tone-on-tone print for place mat centers and napkins
- 1 yard 45-inch-wide polyester fleece
- ¼-inch-wide fusible web
- Leaf embroidery design of your choice
- Polyester or rayon embroidery thread in fall colors for leaves
- Water-soluble liquid stabilizer
- Sewing machine with computerized embroidery unit and hoop
- Serger
- Basic sewing supplies and equipment

Cutting
Note: Preshrink the fabrics before cutting the pieces.

From the rust fabric for place mat centers and napkins:
- Cut four 18-inch squares for the napkins.
- Cut four 6½ x 12½-inch rectangles for center panels.
- Cut four 12½ x 18½-inch rectangles for backing.

From the brown fabric for borders:
- Cut six 4½ x 40-inch strips; subcut strips into eight each 4½ x 6½-inch and 4½ x 20½-inch strips for borders. **Note:** *These strips are cut wider than necessary; you will trim them to size after embroidering the assembled place mat panels.*

From the polyester fleece:
- Cut four 12½ x 18½-inch rectangles.

Place Mat Assembly
All seam allowances are ¼ inch wide.

1. Sew a short border strip to each short edge of each place mat center. Press.

2. Add a long border strip to the top and bottom edges of each place mat center (Figure 1). Press.

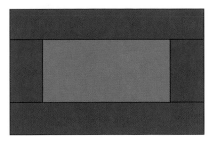

Figure 1

3. Apply liquid stabilizer to each place mat front and allow to dry. Apply stabilizer to one corner of each napkin square in an area that measures approximately 6 inches square. Allow to dry. Press.

4. Load the embroidery design into the embroidery unit. Two sets of leaves are required at the long seam lines and only one set at the short seam lines. Choose several different leaf embroideries and combine them to make your own design for the place mats and napkins.

5. Mark the centers for each leaf design at each place mat seam line, remembering to mirror-image the designs for the opposite borders.

6. Complete the embroideries on each place mat and remove the stabilizer following the package directions. Dry and press.

7. Trim border on each place mat to 3¼ inches wide.

8. Apply a light coat of temporary spray adhesive to one side of each fleece rectangle and smooth in place on the wrong side of a backing rectangle.

9. With right sides together, stitch each place mat to a fleece-backed rectangle, leaving a 5-inch opening in one long edge for turning (Figure 2). *Note: Stitching and pivoting as shown makes it easier to turn in the opening edges for a smooth finish. See Perfect Points & Corners on page 55.* Clip the corners to eliminate bulk and turn the place mat right side out through the opening. Gently shape each corner. Press outer edges so the backing doesn't show.

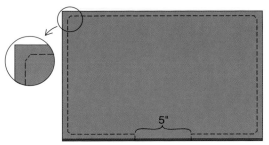

Figure 2

10. Fuse the opening edges together with a strip of fusible web.

Napkin Assembly

1. Mark the embroidery placement in the corner of each napkin square. Baste scrap strips of fabric to the adjacent corners of each napkin square as shown in Figure 3 to make it possible to hoop the fabric for embroidery. Fold each prepared napkin in half diagonally to mark the centerline. Hoop the napkin corner diagonally to complete the embroidery. Do not remove the stabilizer yet.

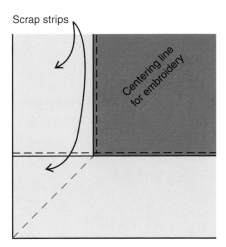

Figure 3

2. Thread the serger with serger thread in the needle and lower looper, and topstitching thread in the upper looper. Adjust the serger for a rolled-edge stitch and test on a fabric scrap. Rolled-edge-finish the raw edges of each napkin. *Note: If you prefer, make a double narrow hem at the napkin edges.*

3. Wash the napkins to remove the stabilizer; press. 🍴

Bee-Dazzled Summer

Design by Carolyn S. Vagts

Do be a do bee and sew this "bee-dazzeled" table runner. It will draw in your guests like bees to honey, and you'll be sure to create a buzz at your next summer occasion.

Finished size
44½ x 18 inches

Materials
- 45-inch-wide fabric:
    - 1 yard cream dot for background, outer border, backing and binding
    - ⅛ yard dark green batik for accent border
    - ⅓ yard cream mottled for diamond backgrounds
- ½ yard thin batting
- Fabric scraps for appliqué*:
    - light green batik
    - dark green batik
    - brown batik
    - gold batik
    - yellow batik
    - black solid
- Fusible web
- Black #8 pearl cotton
- Basic sewing supplies and equipment

*Scraps of accent border fabric were used for dark green on model project.

Cutting
From fabric for background, outer border and binding:
- Cut one 14½-inch square; subcut square into quarters diagonally making four triangles.
- Cut four 2½-inch strips the width of the fabric for outer border.
- Cut three 2-inch strips the width of the fabric for binding.

Note: Backing will be cut later.

From fabric for accent border:
- Cut three 1-inch strips the width of the fabric.

From diamond background fabric (B):
- Cut three 9½-inch squares.

From fabric scraps for appliqué:
- Apply fusible web to the backs of scraps. Using patterns provided (page 47), cut sunflower petals, sunflower center, extra petals, leaves and ½ x 7-inch strips for stems to make two sunflowers; cut bee body from yellow and bee stripes, head and wings from black to make one bee.

Note: Stems can be made using a wide satin stitch, if preferred.

Assembly

Use ¼-inch-wide seam allowances unless otherwise stated.

1. Sew one quarter-square triangle to one 9½-inch square (Figure 1). Make two units.

Figure 1

2. Sew a quarter-square triangle to each side of the remaining 9½-inch square (Figure 2). Make one unit. Press.

Figure 2

3. Sew units from steps 1 and 2 together (Figure 3). Press.

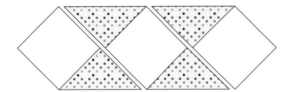

Figure 3

4. Sew the 1-inch-wide accent border to each of the long sides, leaving extra length to trim to maintain shape before adding the two end pieces of accent border. Press. Sew accent border to ends, trimming in same manner. Press.

5. Sew outer border strips to long sides and then to end points in same manner as accent border (Figure 4). Press.

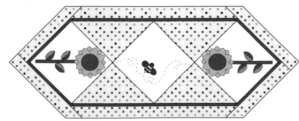

Figure 4

6. Referring to photo, arrange sunflowers and bee in diamond triangles and fuse in place. *Note: Slip extra petals behind sunflower petals before fusing.*

7. Cut backing to fit runner. Sandwich batting between runner and backing. Stitch around edges of appliqué and stitch-in-the-ditch to quilt.

8. Using ⅝-inch seam allowance (and trimming seam to ⅜ inch), bind edges of runner with 2-inch-wide strips.

9. Make running stitch with black pearl cotton to create bee trail.

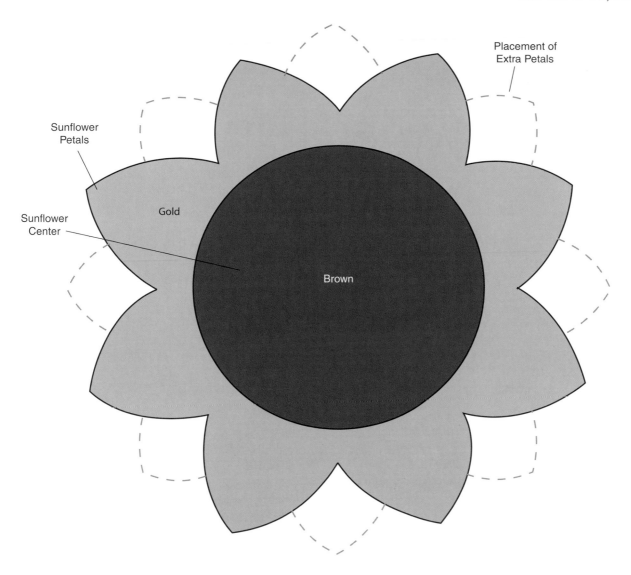

Placement of
Extra Petals

Sunflower
Petals

Sunflower
Center

Gold

Brown

**Bee-Dazzled Summer
Sunflower**

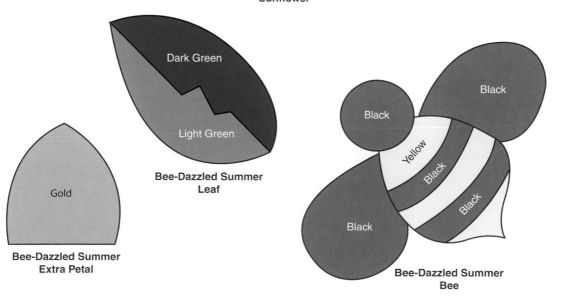

Dark Green

Light Green

**Bee-Dazzled Summer
Leaf**

Gold

**Bee-Dazzled Summer
Extra Petal**

Black

Black

Yellow

Black

Black

Black

**Bee-Dazzled Summer
Bee**

A Halloween Harvest

Designs by Janis Bullis

A rich, autumn-inspired reversible place mat dresses the table from Halloween through Thanksgiving. A jack-o'-lantern on one side and autumnal pumpkin on the other lets you decorate in style throughout the season.

Finished size
18 x 14 inches

Materials for Double Sided Place Mat
- ½ yard 45-inch-wide gold or yellow mediumweight quilting fabric for background
- ¾ yard 45-inch-wide green mediumweight quilting fabric for border*
- Mediumweight 45-inch-wide quilting fabric for appliqués:
    - ½ yard bright orange for jack-o'-lantern and candy
    - ½ yard subdued orange for pumpkin
    - ⅛ yard burgundy for leaves
    - ⅛ yard brown for facial features
    - ⅛ yard yellow for candy
    - ⅛ yard white for candy
- 1 yard mediumweight, nonwoven fusible interfacing
- 2 yards paper-backed fusible web
- Basic sewing supplies and equipment

*Stems for pumpkins were cut from a scrap of border fabric.

Cutting
From background fabric and fusible interfacing:
- Cut two 14 x 18-inch rectangles each. Fuse interfacing rectangles to wrong sides of fabric rectangles.

From border fabric:
- Cut two strips on the bias, each 4 inches wide by approximately 40 inches long.

From appliqué fabric:
- Working with general shapes ½ to 1 inch larger than pattern pieces (page 51), fuse paper-backed fusible web to wrong side of each fabric color as shown in Figure 1.

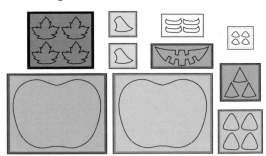

Figure 1

Trace pattern on paper side of fusible web and cut out; remove paper backing.

Assembly

1. Position pumpkin and stem appliqués on background pieces; fuse in place. ***Note:*** *Pumpkins should be centered on background and at least 1½ inches from cut edges.*

2. Set sewing machine for satin-stitch and attach appliqué foot. Satin-stitch all edges of stems and pumpkins.

3. Position, fuse and satin-stitch candy, facial features and leaf appliqués, leaving at least 1½ inches of space along cut edges of background fabric.

4. With wrong sides together, pin and baste edges of appliquéd rectangles together ½ inch from cut edges.

5. Bind edges of place mat with border strips, making a 1-inch-wide border with mitered corners as shown in Figure 2.

Figure 2

Tip

Select the background and border fabrics first; then choose bright colors for the accent appliqués on the Halloween side and more subdued autumn colors for the harvest side.

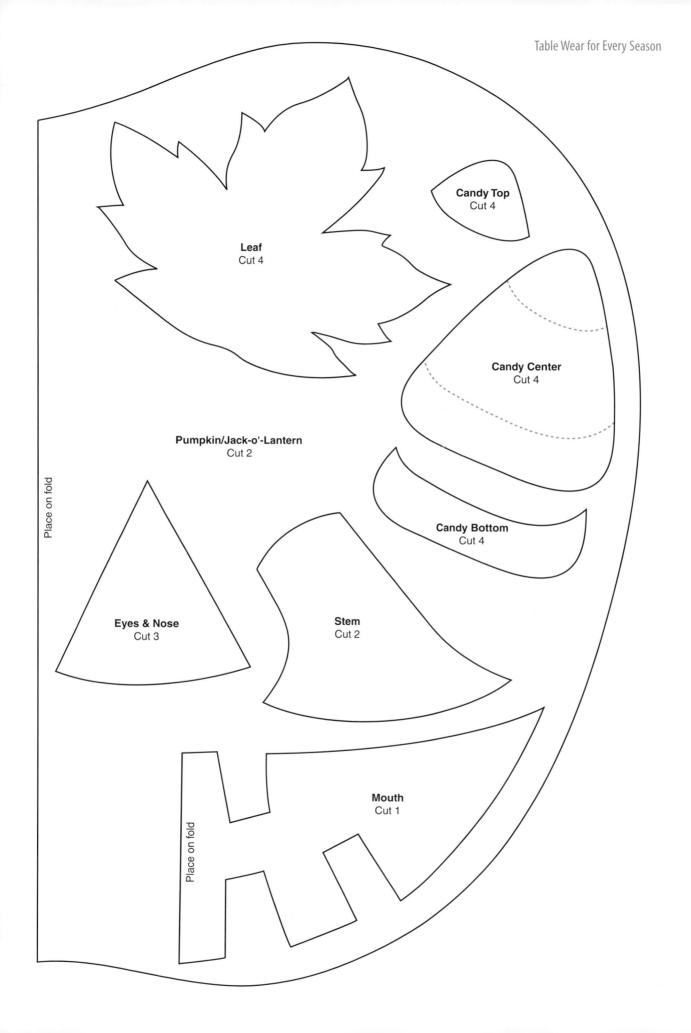

Candy Top
Cut 4

Leaf
Cut 4

Candy Center
Cut 4

Pumpkin/Jack-o'-Lantern
Cut 2

Candy Bottom
Cut 4

Place on fold

Eyes & Nose
Cut 3

Stem
Cut 2

Mouth
Cut 1

Place on fold

Fall Foliage

Designs by Pam Archer

Fall into fall fashion with this autumn-inspired place setting. Use warm colors and crisp fabrics for a seasonal look.

Finished sizes
Place Mat: 12 x 20 inches
Napkin Wrap: 17 x 17 inches

Materials for set of four
• 44/45-inch-wide fabric:
  2 yards brocade (fall-leaf color or your choice) for the place mat fronts and backs
  1½ yards coordinating taffeta for napkin wraps and contrast vein on place mats
• 4 (18–20-inch-square) ready-made linen napkins in a matching or contrasting color
• 10-inch square each 3 coordinating fabrics for the napkin-ring decor
• 4 napkin rings in a rustic theme and color to coordinate with fall leaves
• 4 yards 2-inch-wide sheer organdy ribbon for the napkin-ring decor
• 2 yards 44/45-inch-wide fusible interfacing
• 1 yard lightweight cotton batting
• ¼ yard 24-inch-wide double-sided fusible heavyweight nonwoven stabilizer
• Pattern tracing cloth or paper
• Template plastic
• 2 yards 20-gauge florist's wire
• Short sprigs dried eucalyptus or other fall foliage
• Wire cutters or craft scissors
• Basic sewing supplies and equipment

Cutting
From brocade:
Enlarge the place mat leaf and vein pattern (Figure 1) on pattern tracing cloth and cut out.
• Fold brocade in half with right sides out and selvages aligned. Cut four pairs of place mat leaves for place mat fronts and backs.

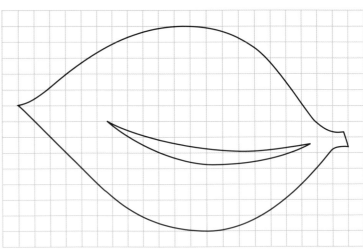

Figure 1
Place Mat Pattern
1 square = 1"

From coordinating taffeta:
• Cut four 19-inch squares for napkin wraps.
• On remaining taffeta, place the vein pattern on the bias grain of fabric. Trace pattern to make four veins. Cut out.

From 10-inch squares coordinating fabrics for napkin-ring decor:
• Cut each square in half to make six 5 x 10-inch rectangles. Pair and fuse together rectangles of different colors. Using patterns for napkin-ring leaves (page 54), cut one set of three leaves from each rectangle.

From fusible interfacing:
• From a double thickness of interfacing, cut four pairs of place mat leaves. *Note: If cutting from a single layer, be sure to cut four and four reversed.*

From cotton batting:
• Cut four place mat leaf shapes.

From organdy ribbon:
• Cut four 1-yard pieces.

From florist's wire:
• Cut 12 (8-inch) pieces.

Place Mat Assembly

Use ½-inch-wide seam allowances unless otherwise noted.

1. Following the manufacturer's instructions, fuse an interfacing leaf to the wrong side of each place mat leaf.

2. Pin a piece of cotton batting to the wrong side of each of the four place mat fronts; machine-baste ⅜ inch from the raw edges. Trim the batting close to the stitching.

3. Machine-baste ¼ inch from the outer edge of each leaf vein. Turn under and press ¼ inch along the basting, allowing the basting stitches to roll to the underside so they are not visible on the front. Trim excess fabric at the points to eliminate bulk.

4. Center a vein on each place mat front and pin in place. Stitch along the outer edges of each vein.

5. *Note: See Perfect Points & Corners, page 55.* With right sides together and raw edges aligned, pin each place mat front to a back. Stitch around the outer edges, leaving a 4-inch-long opening along the lower curved edge for turning. Use pinking shears to trim the seam allowances and notch out the fullness in the curves at the same time.

6. Turn each place mat right side out through the opening and press. Turn in the opening edges and slipstitch together.

Easy Basting

When layering batting and backing for place mats, apply a light coat of temporary spray adhesive to one side of the batting rectangle, and then smooth into place on the backing rectangle. This eliminates pinning and helps prevent the layers from shifting while you stitch the batting in place.

Napkin Wrap & Ring Assembly

Use ½-inch-wide seam allowances unless otherwise noted.

1. On each taffeta napkin-wrap square, turn under and press a scant ½ inch; turn and press again. Clip corners to eliminate bulk. Refold and topstitch in place close to the inner folded edges.

2. Adjust the sewing machine for a narrow satin stitch and stitch over the raw edges of napkin-ring leaves to finish.

3. Position a piece of florist's wire in the center of each leaf, with the upper end about one third of the length of the leaf from the tip. Attach an open-toe appliqué foot to your sewing machine and position the leaf between the toes of the foot. Satin-stitch over the wire and continue satin-stitching over the wire slightly beyond the leaf as well (Figure 2).

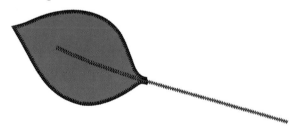

Figure 2

4. Select one leaf of each size and twist the wire stems together tightly. Wrap each set of leaves around a napkin ring and secure by twisting the ends around the base of the leaves. Cut away excess wire. Arrange the leaves as desired.

5. Tuck a sprig of eucalyptus or other fall foliage under the wires and glue in place. Slip a length of ribbon through the ring and tie in a square knot or a bow. Trim the ribbon ends to the desired length, cutting at an angle to prevent fraying.

6. Fold the linen napkins in quarters and tuck inside the taffeta napkin wraps. Tuck through a completed napkin ring and arrange so the napkin points show.

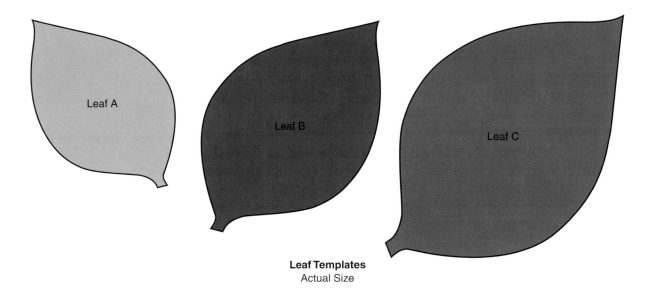

Leaf Templates
Actual Size

Perfect Points & Corners

Enclosed points and corners like the ones in the Fall Foliage place mats will be more stable and turn more squarely, or to a better point, if you use this neat stitching trick.

1. As you approach a square corner or a point, stop stitching 1 inch from it and adjust the stitch length to 15–18 stitches per inch.

2. Stitch to the corner or the point, ending one stitch shy of the actual corner. Stop and raise the presser foot.

3. Pivot the work halfway and take two short stitches across the corner (or three across a very sharp point) rather than making a complete pivot at the point or corner. Complete the pivot, stitch for the next inch and then stop to change the stitch length to normal (Figure 3).

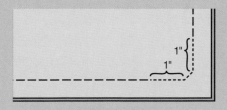

Figure 3

4. Repeat the process at each corner or point. Trim the seams, turn the piece right side out and press.

Note: *To avoid poking a hole in the corners, use a wooden or plastic point turner to smooth out the corners before pressing. A wooden chopstick or a knitting needle with a blunt point may be substituted.*

Why does this stitching trick result in smoother corners? The stitches across the point allow a little more room to accommodate the trimmed corner layers inside the turned edge.

Finely Feathered

Designs by Pam Archer

Feast your eyes with these fun feathered place mats and napkin rings. These will be sure to ruffle some feathers at your next gathering.

Finished sizes
Place Mat: 20 inches in diameter
Napkin: 17 x 17 inches
Napkin Ring: 2 inches in diameter

Materials for set of four
• 3¾ yards 44/45-inch-wide brown or tan linen for place mats and napkins
• 1 yard 44/45-inch-wide lightweight fusible interfacing
• 1 yard lightweight cotton batting
• 9 yards 5-inch-wide feather trim on header
• 1 yard ⅞-inch-wide brown velvet ribbon
• Basic sewing supplies and equipment

Cutting
From linen fabric:
• Cut four 19-inch squares for the napkins.
• Cut eight 16-inch circles for place mat fronts and backs.

From batting:
• Cut four 16-inch circles.

From interfacing:
• Cut four 16-inch circles.

From feather trim:
• Cut one 45-inch-long and one 27-inch-long piece for each place mat.
• Cut two 5-inch-long pieces for each napkin ring.

From velvet ribbon:
• Cut four 9-inch lengths.

Place Mat Assembly
Use ½-inch-wide seam allowances unless otherwise directed.

1. Following the manufacturer's directions, fuse the interfacing to the wrong side of four of the linen circles for place mat fronts.

2. Position a batting circle on the wrong side of each remaining linen circle for place mat backs. Machine-baste ⅜ inch from the raw edges and trim the batting close to the stitching.

Note: Refer to Figure 1 for steps 3–6.

3. With the interfacing and batting sides facing each other, pin together place mat fronts and backs with raw edges aligned. Machine-baste across the center of each pair. Trim edges even if needed.

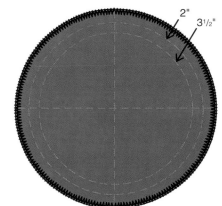

2"
3½"

Figure 1

4. Adjust the sewing machine for a wide, closely spaced satin stitch, and satin-stitch over the raw edges around each mat. Press.

5. On each mat, use a fabric marker to draw a positioning line 2 inches from the outer edge, and a second line 3½ inches from the outer edge.

6. Position the header of the 45-inch-long piece of feather trim along the outer line and pin in place. The outer tips of the feathers should extend about 2 inches beyond the satin-stitched edge. Machine-stitch the header to the place mat. Cut away excess trim as needed. Position the 27-inch length along the inner line; pin, stitch in place and trim as needed.

Optional: If you want to set the table with place mats and napkins in rings without dinnerware in place (for a buffet, for example), cut a center circle out of matching or contrasting nonwoven synthetic suede or wool felt to cover the feather header. Make it large enough in diameter to completely cover the header so it won't show. Machine-stitch in place around the outer edge or use permanent fabric adhesive to glue it in place.

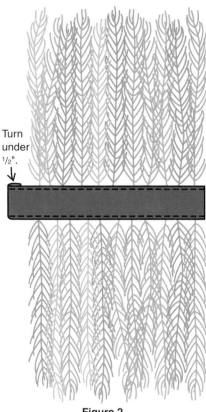

Turn under ½".

Figure 2

Napkin & Napkin Ring Assembly

1. On each linen napkin square, turn under and press a scant ½ inch; then turn and press again. Clip corners to eliminate bulk. Refold and topstitch in place close to the inner folded edges.

Note: Refer to Figure 2 for steps 2 and 3.

2. For each napkin ring, overlap the headers of two 5-inch lengths of feather trim. Machine-baste through the header centers.

3. Center the feather trim on a length of velvet ribbon, facedown, and pin in place. From the right side, stitch along each outer edge of the ribbon to attach it to the feathers. Trim excess ribbon 1 inch from each end of the feather trim. Turn under one end and hand- or machine-tack in place. Turn under and tack ½ inch at the opposite ribbon end, creating an extension.

4. To form ring, lap the turned edge over the ribbon extension and hand-stitch the layers together. Tuck the linen napkin into the ring and arrange the points as desired.

Easy-to-Grow Poinsettia

Design by Carolyn S. Vagts

Grow this poinsettia table runner for the holiday season and amaze friends and family with your green thumb. You'll enjoy this carefree poinsettia for years to come.

Finished size
53 x 16½ inches

Materials
• 45-inch-wide fabric for background:
    ½ yard cream A
    ½ yard cream B
• ⅛ yard 45-inch-wide green solid fabric for flange
• 1½ yards 45-inch-wide green print fabric for
    border, backing and binding
• ½ yard thin batting
• Batik fabric scraps for appliqué:
    2 shades red
    2 shades green
• Fusible web
• Buttons for poinsettia centers:
    11 (7⁄16-inch) green
    11 (¼-inch) red
• Basic sewing supplies and equipment

Cutting
From background fabric A:
• Cut one 6⅞-inch square; subcut square into quarters diagonally making four triangles (Figure 1).
• Cut one 3¾-inch square; subcut square in half diagonally making two triangles (Figure 2).
• Cut 13 (4½-inch) squares (A square).

Figure 1   **Figure 2**

From background fabric B:
• Cut 16 (4½-inch) squares (B squares).

From fabric for flange:
• Cut four 1-inch strips the width of the fabric.

From green print fabric for border, backing and binding:
• Cut four 2½-inch-wide strips the width of the fabric for border.
• Cut four 2-inch-wide strips the width of the fabric for binding.
Note: *Backing will be cut later.*

From batik fabric scraps for appliqué:
• Apply fusible web. Using templates provided (page 62), cut petals and leaves to make two poinsettias.

Assembly

Use ¼-inch-wide seam allowances unless otherwise stated.

1. Sew one 4½-inch B square to each end of a 4½-inch A square (Figure 3). Make five units. Press.

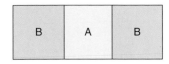

Figure 3

2. Sew one 4½-inch A square to each end of a 4½-inch B square (Figure 4). Make four units. Press.

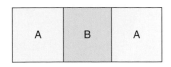

Figure 4

3. Sew one quarter-square triangle to each end of a 4½-inch B square (Figure 5). Make two end units. Press.

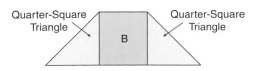

Figure 5

4. Sew units from steps 1 and 2 together alternately to create a checkerboard (Figure 6). Press.

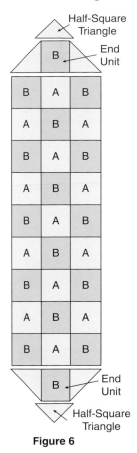

Figure 6

5. Sew a step-3 unit to each end of the checkerboard unit. Press.

6. Sew one half-square triangle to each end of checkerboard to finish points of runner (Figure 6). Press.

7. Fold flange strips in half along length with right sides out; press. Using a scant ¼-inch seam, and with right sides facing, sew flange strips to both long edges of checkerboard unit; then sew flange strips to diagonal ends.

8. Sew the border strips to long edges of runner and trim ends (Figure 7 on page 62). Press. Sew border strips to ends, one at a time, trimming after each piece of border is added to maintain shape. Press.

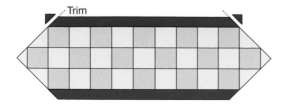

Figure 7

11. Using ⅝-inch seam allowance (and trimming seam to ⅜ inch), bind edges of runner with 2-inch-wide strips. Stack red buttons on green buttons; sew in place for poinsettia centers. 🖊

9. Using the photo as a reference, arrange poinsettias on runner and fuse in place. Cut backing to fit runner, piecing ends if necessary. Sandwich batting between runner and backing.

10. Stitch veins and edges of poinsettia petals and leaves and stitch-in-the-ditch to quilt.

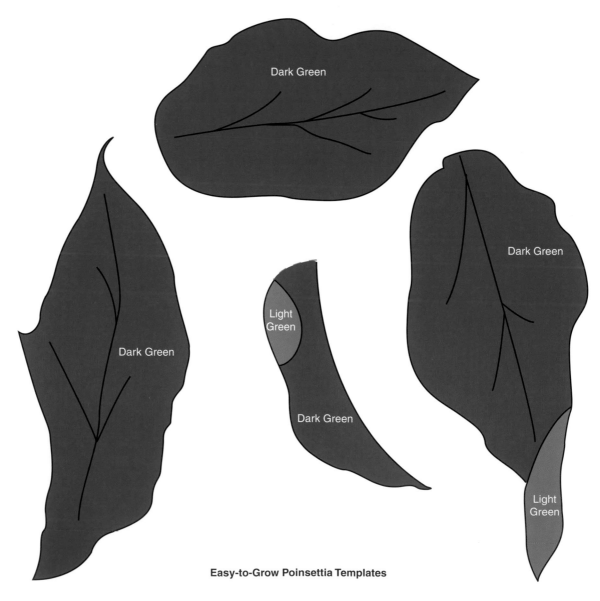

Easy-to-Grow Poinsettia Templates

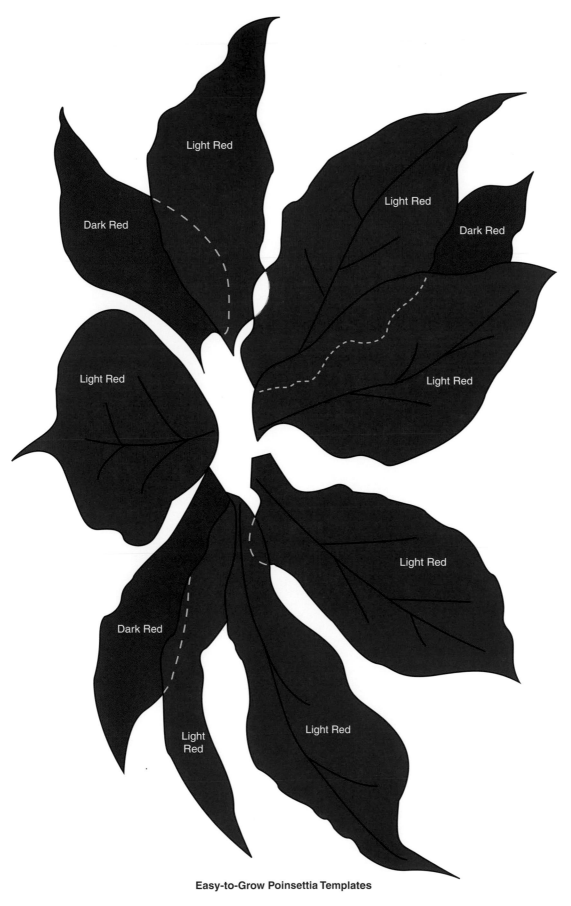

Easy-to-Grow Poinsettia Templates

Make It Merry Mats

Designs by Linda Turner Griepentrog

Embellishing ready-made place mats is a fast and easy way to spruce up your holiday table. Seasonal shapes, fun stitches and quick fusing combine for these fast and easy whimsical mats.

Finished size

13 x 18 inches

Materials

- 4 ready-made rectangular fabric place mats
- Assorted fabric scraps for appliqués
- Assorted trims
- Fusible interfacing
- Paper-backed fusible web
- Optional: water-soluble stabilizer
- Rayon machine-embroidery thread
- Fabric/craft glue
- Optional: decorative-edge scissors
- Basic sewing supplies and equipment, including matching or contrasting thread

Notes: For level table settings, choose smooth fabrics for the appliqués rather than fabrics with textured surfaces. Washable felt, faux suede, cotton broadcloth or poplin are all good choices.

Preshrink place mats and appliqué fabrics to avoid distortion during future launderings.

Fused appliqué fabrics generally don't ravel, but stitching secures them and also adds a decorative element. If you prefer to stitch around the motifs, use a zigzag, blanket stitch or other decorative machine stitch. Use thread in the bobbin to match the place mat color and thread in the needle to match or contrast with the appliqué.

Instructions

1. Back each appliqué fabric with fusible interfacing if more body is needed, or to add opacity if a light-colored appliqué is being applied to a dark-colored place mat.

2. Trace the desired appliqué shapes (page 67) onto the paper side of the fusible web, allowing at least ½ inch between motifs. Cut out each shape with a ¼-inch-wide margin all around.

3. Fuse each appliqué shape to the wrong side of the appropriate appliqué fabric. If you plan to fuse and then stitch around the outer edges of the appliqués, cut out each shape on the drawn lines. If you do not plan to stitch after fusing, consider using decorative-edge scissors to cut out the shapes. Fuse each appliqué on the place mat.

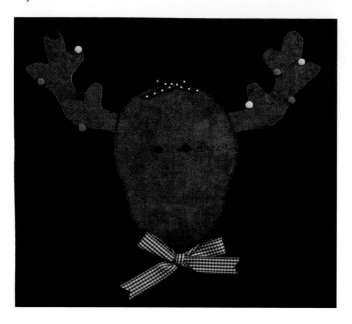

4. If desired, embellish appliqués with decorative machine stitching using a heavyweight water-soluble stabilizer.

5. Add flat trims, buttons, ribbons or sequins, placing away from tableware placement area.

Mat-Making Basics

If you prefer to make your own place mats, follow these easy steps.

1. For each place mat, cut two 14 x 19-inch rectangles of fabric. Back one or both with fusible interfacing for more stability.

2. Embellish the place mat front with appliqués as directed above.

3. With right sides together and using ½-inch-wide seam allowances, sew the two mats together. Leave a 4-inch-long opening in one long edge and pivot at the beginning and end of the opening as shown in Figure 1.

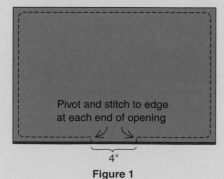

Pivot and stitch to edge
at each end of opening

4"

Figure 1

For smoothly turned corners, stitch to within ½ inch of the corner and then change the stitch length to a short stitch. Continue stitching until you are almost to the pivot point. Pivot and take two stitches across the corner (Figure 2). Pivot, stitch for ½ inch and then return to the normal stitch length until you reach the next corner.

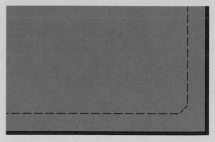

Figure 2

4. Clip the corners and trim the seams to ¼ inch. Turn the mat right side out and hand-stitch the opening closed.

5. Topstitch ¼ inch from the outer edges if desired.

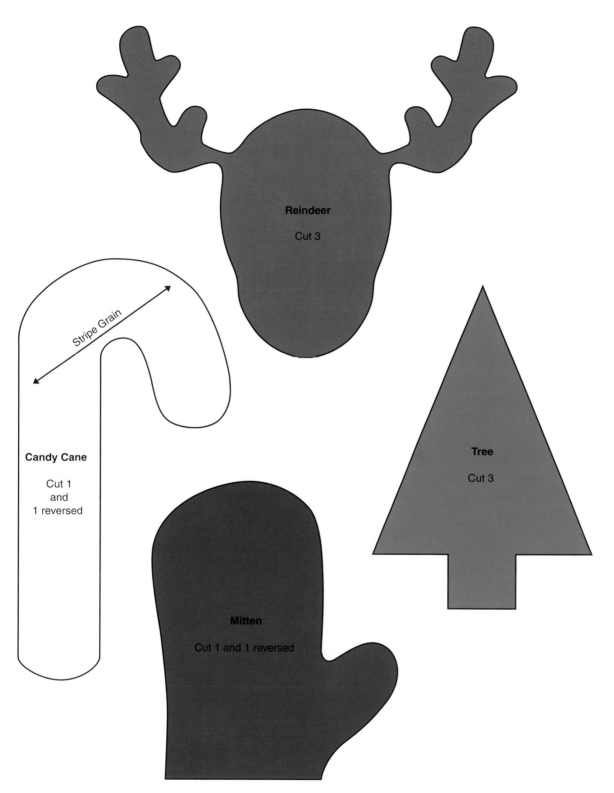

Reindeer

Cut 3

Stripe Grain

Candy Cane

Cut 1
and
1 reversed

Tree

Cut 3

Mitten

Cut 1 and 1 reversed

Templates for Make It Merry Mats
Enlarge 200%

Beading Sensation

Designs by Pam Archer

Bead your way into their hearts with this elegant place mat and gossamer napkin wrap.

Finished sizes
Place Mat: 13 x 19 inches
Napkin Wrap: 17 x 17 inches

Materials for set of four
- 44/45-inch-wide fabrics:
    1 yard beaded satin or other beaded or sequined fabric for the place-mat borders
    2¼ yards polyester satin fabric for the place-mat centers and backing
    1¼ yards polyester or silk organza for the napkin wraps
- 1⅝ yards 36-inch-wide lightweight fusible interfacing (woven, weft-insertion or knit)
- 1⅝ yards lightweight cotton batting
- 4 (12-inch-long) pieces silver wire-edge ribbon
- Optional: temporary spray adhesive
- Spray-on fabric protector
- Large white or gray linen, or white or silvery paper napkins
- Basic sewing supplies and equipment

Cutting
From beaded fabric:
- Cut four 14 x 20-inch rectangles. From the center of each, mark and cut out an 8 x 14-inch rectangle to form a frame for place mat borders (Figure 1).

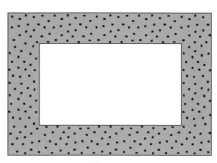

Figure 1

From satin fabric:
- Cut four 10 x 16-inch rectangles for the place mat centers.
- Cut four 14 x 20-inch rectangles for place mat backs.

From organza:
- Cut four 19-inch squares for napkin wraps.

From fusible interfacing:
- Cut four 14 x 20-inch rectangles. From the center of each, mark and cut out an 8 x 14-inch rectangle for border interfacings.

From the cotton batting:
- Cut four 14 x 20-inch rectangles.

Assembly

Use ½-inch-wide seam allowances unless otherwise directed.

1. Fuse an 8 x 14-inch interfacing cutout to the wrong side of each 10 x 16-inch satin rectangle for the place mat centers.

2. Apply the interfacing borders to wrong sides of beaded borders. *Note: Test iron heat and fusing method on scraps first. If fusing doesn't work or damages the fabric, substitute a woven fabric and machine-baste in place ⅜ inch from all raw edges.*

3. Position a batting rectangle on the wrong side of each 14 x 20-inch satin rectangle. Machine-baste ⅜ inch from the raw edges and trim the excess batting close to the stitching.

4. Turn under and press ½ inch on each edge of each 10 x 16-inch satin rectangle for the place mat centers. Center and pin a satin center, right side up, on the right side of each place mat frame. Edge-stitch in place (Figure 2 on page 70) to complete the front of each place mat.

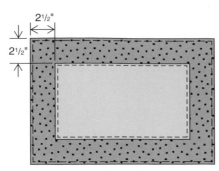

2½"

2½"

Figure 2

5. With right sides facing, pin a place mat front to a back. Stitch, leaving a 4-inch opening in the center of one long edge for turning. Clip corners and trim seam allowances to ¼ inch to reduce bulk. Turn right side out through the opening and press, using a press cloth as needed to protect the fabrics. Turn in the opening edges and slip-stitch together.

6. On each organza napkin-wrap square, turn under and press a scant ½ inch; turn and press

again. Clip corners to eliminate bulk. Refold and topstitch in place close to the inner folded edges.

Optional: *For a more festive touch, finish the napkin wraps with serged rolled edges using metallic thread in the upper looper. Test on scraps first.*

7. In lieu of napkin rings, gather napkins inside sheer napkin wraps and tie with wire-edge ribbon. Trim each ribbon end at an angle. 🍴

Marinated Shrimp Relish

You may serve this mélange on lettuce or as a cocktail.

3 pounds cleaned, cooked shrimp
2 cups minced onions
2 cups snipped fresh parsley
1⅓ cups extra-virgin olive oil
⅔ cup vinegar
2 cloves garlic, minced
1 tablespoon salt
Pinch pepper

In large bowl, combine shrimp, onions and parsley. In mixing bowl, combine olive oil, vinegar, garlic, salt and pepper. Beat well. Pour over shrimp mixture. Chill for at least 1 hour before serving or overnight. Serves 8.

Casual Table Wear

Making your own designer table wear is fun, easy and fast. You can dress your table in styles suitable for any occasion, from casual dining inspired by your local bistro, to styles for carefree summer picnicking, or try your hand at playful styles for your child's birthday party.

Coming Up Flowers Table Runner

Design by Carol Zentgraf

Create a tabletop garden with this pretty runner made from wool felt. These wool-felt flowers are sew easy to grow, you'll have the garden of your dreams in no time.

Finished size
15 x 72 inches

Materials
• 36-inch-wide wool felt:
    2 yards each pistachio ice cream #0703 and white #1100
    ½ yard each lemon #0417, cotton candy #0905, English rose #0944, mulberry #0966, robin's egg #0580, periwinkle #0581, Norwegian blue #0579 and chartreuse #0715
• Permanent fabric adhesive
• Basic sewing supplies and equipment

Cutting
From pistachio ice cream felt:
• Cut two 3½ x 72-inch strips for side borders.
• Cut two 3½ x 15-inch strips for end borders.

From white felt:
• Cut one 9 x 66-inch rectangle for center.

From lemon, cotton candy, English rose, mulberry, robin's egg, periwinkle and Norwegian blue:
• Use flower pattern provided to cut 10 flowers from each color.

From chartreuse felt:
• Use the leaf pattern provided to cut 90–100 leaves.

Assembly
Use ½-inch seam allowances.

1. Center and sew side border strips to long edges of center panel, beginning and ending ½ inch from corners (Figure 1).

Figure 1

2. Sew end border strips to short edges of center–border unit in same manner.

3. To miter border strips at each corner, fold the corner with right sides together and the strip ends even; pin together. Mark a line from the outer corner of the strip end to the stitching line (Figure 2). Stitch along the line; trim the excess felt ½ inch from the stitching. Press all seams open.

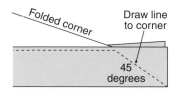

Figure 2

4. Referring to Figure 3, shape each flower by folding in half and then folding in each side, overlapping slightly. Zigzag-stitch across the base of the folded flower to secure.

5. Apply a thin layer of fabric adhesive to the lower half of one leaf and wrap it around the base of a flower, covering the flower

Fold in half

Fold in right side

Fold in left side

Figure 3

end. Hold tightly for several seconds until securely attached. Repeat for each leaf and each flower. Randomly add a second leaf to several flowers of each color.

6. Referring to photo for placement, arrange and glue flowers with leaves around the table runner border as desired. ❦

Sources: WoolFelt felt from National Nonwovens; Fabri-Tac permanent fabric adhesive from Beacon Adhesives.

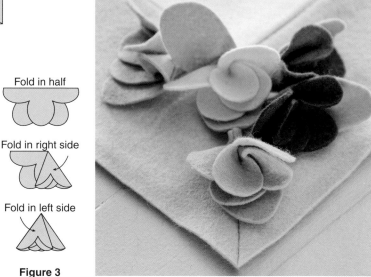

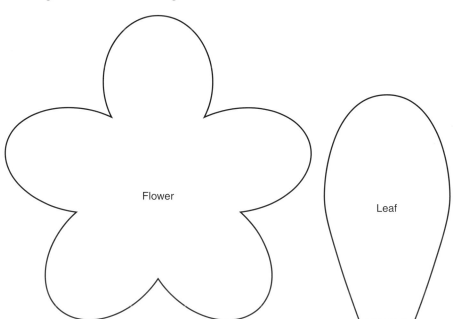

Coming Up Flowers Table Runner Patterns

Bali Tablecloth

Design by Lucy A. Fazely & Michael L. Burns

Capture the beautiful colors of falling leaves with a selection of batik fabrics. The appliquéd leaf shapes scattered around the table topper will dress up your autumn decor.

Finished size
41 x 41 inches

Materials
• 44/45-inch-wide fabrics:
  - 1¼ yards cream batik
  - 8 fat eighths batik prints in fall colors for appliqués
• Template plastic or thin, sturdy cardboard
• 1¼ yards 12-inch-wide fusible web
• ⅔ yard 20-inch-wide tear-away stabilizer
• Basic sewing supplies and equipment

Tablecloth
1. Fold the 1¼-yard piece of cream batik in half lengthwise. Fold in half again crosswise (Figure 1).

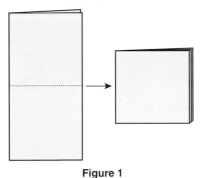

Figure 1

2. Trim the folded fabric to measure 21 x 21 inches (Figure 2). Cut the excess from the selvage and raw edges only. Do not cut at the folded edges. **Note:** *If the fabric is not wide enough to trim to this size, trim to 20 x 20 inches instead.*

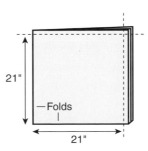

21"

—Folds

21"

Figure 2

3. With the fabric square still folded, mark and cut away a 12¼-inch triangle at the corner with the cut edges (Figure 3). ***Note:*** *Cut away an 11¾-inch triangle if your trimmed square is only 20 x 20 inches.*

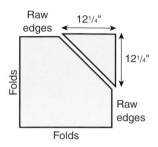

Figure 3

4. Turn under, press and stitch a narrow finished hem on all edges of tablecloth.

5. Fold the tablecloth into eighths and press to mark the sections. Open the tablecloth (Figure 4).

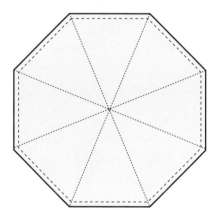

Figure 4

Leaf Appliqués

1. On the paper side of the fusible web, trace around the leaf template 16 times. Leave ½ inch of space between shapes. Reverse the template and trace 16 more leaves (32 leaves total).

2. Cut out the leaves in groups of four. Remove the backing paper and fuse the groups on the wrong sides of the appliqué fabrics. Cut out each leaf on the traced lines.

3. Referring to the photo, arrange the leaves in four alternating sections of the tablecloth. Place five leaves above the hemmed edge in each

section and three falling leaves in the area above each five-leaf group. Pin each leaf in place.

4. Lightly fuse the leaves in place. Remove pins and cover leaves with a press cloth to protect the iron. Fuse leaves permanently in place following the manufacturer's directions.

5. Position a piece of tear-away stabilizer under each leaf on the wrong side of the tablecloth and pin in place.

6. Set the machine for a short, narrow zigzag stitch. Machine-appliqué each leaf in place. Use the same stitch setting to embroider the stem/vein on each leaf. For emphasis, zigzag again over the first stem/vein stitching in each leaf. Remove the tear-away stabilizer. 🖴

Leaf Template

Cut It Out:
A Tablecloth Makeover

Design by Carol Zentgraf

Cutwork is so simple and so affordable when you start with a purchased table linen. Embroider, cut and enjoy the envious glances at your next party.

Finished size
Model project measures 50 x 52 inches

Materials
• Purchased tablecloth
• Machine-embroidery design for cutwork
• Water-soluble stabilizer
• Rayon machine-embroidery thread
• Machine-embroidery bobbin thread
• Small sharp curved embroidery scissors
• Sewing machine with embroidery capabilities
• Machine-embroidery hoop
• Basic sewing supplies and equipment

Instructions
1. To mark the diagonal center of one corner of the tablecloth, fold corner in half and press with wrong sides together and hemmed edges even.

2. Open the folded corner. Place stabilizer on the wrong side of the area to be embroidered. Hoop the corner and stabilizer in the machine-embroidery hoop, centering the crease line and

positioning the corner so the design will be approximately 5–6 inches from the corner (Figure 1).

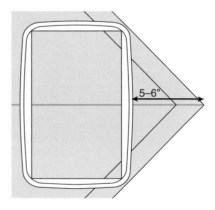

Figure 1

3. With bobbin thread in bobbin and rayon thread in needle, embroider design to the end of the first color stop, or as otherwise indicated by embroidery-design manufacturer. **Note:** *Generally, the first color will stitch an outline of the design with a double line around the areas to be cut out.*

4. Remove hoop from the machine, but do not remove the fabric from the hoop. Using small curved embroidery scissors, carefully cut away the fabric only in the designated cutwork areas. Do not cut through the stabilizer. Cut close to, but not into the stitching lines.

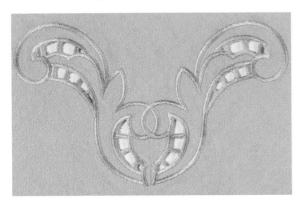

5. Reattach the hoop to the machine and continue stitching to complete the embroidery design.

6. Remove the fabric from the hoop and cut away excess stabilizer. Using warm water, gently rub the remaining stabilizer to remove. Trim threads as needed, being careful not to cut into the embroidery threads.

7. Repeat steps 1–6 to embroider a design in each corner of the tablecloth. 🥄

Sources: Fabri-Solvy stabilizer, Blendables rayon machine-embroidery thread and bobbin thread from Sulky of America; cutwork machine-embroidery design from *Machine Embroidery Room by Room* by Carol Zentgraf, available from Honeybee Studios.

Key Lime Dessert

Make sweet dessert for a delightful ending to any meal.

2 cups crushed graham crackers
½ cup margarine, melted
1½ (14-ounce) cans sweetened condensed milk
4 egg yolks
1 cup lime juice
1 (8-ounce) container frozen whipped topping, thawed

Preheat oven to 350 degrees.
Combine graham cracker crumbs and margarine; mix well. Press into 9 x 9 x 2-inch pan. Combine sweetened condensed milk, egg yolks and lime juice. Pour over crust. Bake 20 minutes or till set. Cool for ½ hour. Top with whipped topping. Serves 9.

Ribbons Galore

Designs by Carol Zentgraf

Nothing says excessive like these beautifully beribboned place mats, napkins and rings. Easy to sew, simply purchase ribbons for enhancement and enjoy.

Finished sizes
Place Mat: 19½ x 13 inches
Napkin: 18 x 18 inches
Napkin Ring: Approximately 17 inches long

Materials for one place mat
• ½ yard 45-inch-wide white cotton fabric
• ½ yard heavyweight fusible interfacing
• Ribbons:
    8 yards total assorted ¼–¾-inch-wide
      for top
    2¾ yards ¾-inch-wide for edges
• Self-adhesive double-sided basting tape
• Clear gridded quilter's ruler
• Invisible thread
• Basic sewing supplies and equipment

Cutting
From white cotton fabric:
• Cut two 19 x 14-inch rectangles.

From interfacing:
• Cut two 19 x 14-inch rectangles.

Assembly
1. Follow manufacturer's directions to fuse interfacing to the wrong side of the cotton-fabric rectangles.

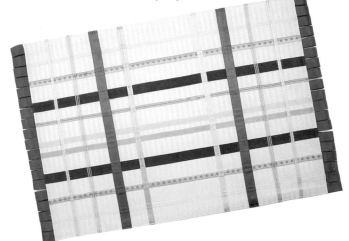

2. Cut assorted-width ribbons into eight 14-inch lengths for vertical strips and nine 19-inch lengths for horizontal strips. Referring to photo for placement, arrange ribbons on right side of one cotton rectangle, keeping top and bottom horizontal ribbons 1½ inches from edges.

3. Center and adhere a strip of double-sided basting tape to the wrong side of each ribbon length. Using the clear ruler to keep strips straight and parallel to the edges, adhere horizontal strips first and then the vertical strips.

4. With white all-purpose thread in the bobbin and invisible thread in the needle, stitch the center of each narrow ribbon strip in place. For each wider-ribbon strip, stitch along both edges.

5. From ¾-inch-wide ribbon for edges, cut 38 lengths each 2½ inches long. On the right side of the ribbon-embellished rectangle, place a piece of basting tape along each short edge, ¼ inch from the edge. Adhere 2½-inch-long ribbons evenly spaced across ends of place mat, with ribbon end overlapping place mat edge ¼ inch. Place a second layer of basting tape across each short edge of the place mat as before, over ribbon ends; then fold the ribbon strips in half with ends even (Figure 1).

Figure 1

6. Press under top and bottom edges of each place mat rectangle ½ inch. Use basting tape to

adhere rectangles together with right sides out and edges even. Edge-stitch panels together using invisible thread.

Napkin

Materials for one napkin
- 19-inch square cotton fabric in desired color
- 2¼ yards ¼-inch-wide ribbon
- Rayon machine-embroidery thread
- Basic sewing supplies and equipment

Assembly
1. Press under edges of fabric ¼ inch. Press under ¼ inch again and edge-stitch hem in place using matching all-purpose thread.

2. With rayon machine-embroidery thread and a long, narrow zigzag stitch, stitch ribbon around edges of napkin over edge stitching.

Afternoon Tea

A casual look for a classic tea. Enjoy your afternoon of elegance.

1. Fold the napkin into quarters (Figure 1).

2. With the loose edges facing up, fold up the bottom corner one third to one half of the way to the top corner (Figure 2).

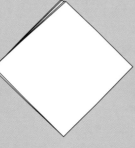

Figure 1

Figure 2

3. Fold in the sides so the napkin is in thirds (Figure 3).

4. Turn the napkin over and lay flat.

Figure 3

Napkin Ring

Materials for one napkin ring

- ½ yard 1½-inch-wide
  sheer ribbon
- 1½-inch-diameter
  sequin flower
- Permanent fabric adhesive
- Seam sealant

Assembly

1. Tie a knot in the center of the ribbon.

2. Glue center back of flower to knot using permanent fabric adhesive.

3. Apply seam sealant to cut ends of ribbon. Let dry.

Sources: Self-adhesive double-sided basting tape from Prym Consumer USA; threads from Sulky of America; ribbons from Offray and Mokuba; sequin flower from Expo International; Fabri-Tac permanent fabric adhesive from Beacon Adhesives.

Summer Bright Tablecloth

Design by Lynn Weglarz

Cover your picnic table with this bright idea for a tablecloth. Store plates, utensils and other picnic necessities in the pockets and keep the cloth from blowing away. Or stitch buttons to each corner and hang a weighted tassel to keep your tablecloth in place.

Finished size
52½ x 93 inches

Materials
- 54-inch-wide woven fabric:
    - 3 yards bright print for tablecloth and binding
    - ⅜ yard coordinating solid for pockets
- 1-inch bias tape maker
- Optional: ½-inch paper-backed fusible tape
- Optional for tassels:
    - 4 (1-inch) buttons
    - assorted yarns to match fabric
    - 4 (¾-ounce) fishing weights
    - 3½ x 2½-inch lightweight cardboard
- Basic sewing supplies and equipment

Cutting
From print fabric for tablecloth:
- Cut one 54 x 95-inch piece.
- Cut 2-inch strips on the bias the width of the fabric to make 105-inch length when joined.

From coordinating solid fabric for pockets:
- Cut two 6-inch strips the width of the fabric.

Assembly
Use ¼-inch seam allowance throughout.

1. Sew together bias strips (Figure 1). Trim and press seams. Pull strip through bias tape maker (Figure 2), pressing with iron as you pull it through, to make 105 inches of bias tape. Favor-press tape to make one side a bit wider than the other (Figure 3).

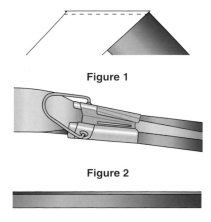

Figure 1

Figure 2

Figure 3

2. With wider side of bias tape on the wrong side, sew bias tape to one long edge of each 6-inch-wide strip of solid fabric for pocket.

3. Place each pocket on one end of tablecloth with wrong side of pocket against right side of tablecloth and raw edges even. Pin and baste.

4. Stitch a ½-inch double hem in raw edges. *Option: Fuse paper-backed fusible tape on wrong side of tablecloth along all edges. Peel paper from short sides. Cut out corner fabric (Figure 4), and then fuse edge to tape. Repeat for remaining edges. Turn under fused edge and topstitch in place.*

Figure 4

5. Referring to stitching diagram, stitch to create pockets (Figure 5).

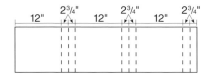

Figure 5

Weighted Tassels (optional)

Note: Make one tassel for each corner of the tablecloth.

1. Thread a 9-inch strand of yarn through one of the fishing weights (Figure 6). Set aside.

Figure 6

2. Wrap remaining yarn around cardboard about five times, or until cardboard has the desired coverage, beginning and ending with yarn ends at bottom of cardboard.

3. Slip end of weighted yarn strand under yarn on cardboard and tie off at the top (Figure 7). Tie ends of weighted yarn to form a top loop for attaching to tablecloth. Trim close to knot.

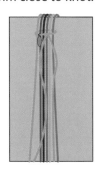

Figure 7

4. Cut loops at bottom of cardboard. Tie another length of yarn around tassel to create the head of the tassel. *Note: The top of the fishing weight should be in this head.* Trim ends of tassel as desired.

5. Sew a button to each corner of the tablecloth. Attach tassels by slipping loops over buttons. ♥

Sources: Steam-A-Seam fusible tape from The Warm Company.

A Pompom Party Table Topper

Design by Janis Bullis

Create a party atmosphere with this custom-made tablecloth. Ensure a perfect table fit by following these simple instructions. Colorful appliquéd gift boxes, pompom trim and grosgrain-ribbon bows will entice guests of all ages.

Finished size
Size varies
Model project measures 60 x 80 inches

Materials
- Medium-weight cotton fabric for tablecloth: amount to be determined
- 11-inch squares brightly colored, medium-weight quilting fabric for appliqués: amount to be determined
- 10-inch squares paper-backed fusible web: amount to be determined
- 11-inch squares medium-weight nonwoven fusible interfacing: amount to be determined
- ½-yard lengths ⅞-inch-wide grosgrain ribbon to coordinate with quilt-fabric squares: amount to be determined
- Pompom-fringe trim to equal finished tablecloth perimeter

- Optional: medium safety pins for attaching ribbon bows
- Pattern paper
- Basic sewing supplies and equipment

Pattern Preparation

1. Measure the length and width of the tabletop. For the drop, measure from the top edge of the table to the top of the chair seat (Figure 1).

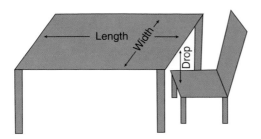

Figure 1

2. For tablecloth width, add the table width plus 2 times the drop measurement plus 2 inches for each hem (a total of 4 inches). For tablecloth length, add the table length plus 2 times the drop measurement plus 2 inches for each hem (for a total of 4 inches) (Figure 2).

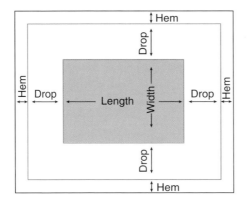

Figure 2

Note: *If tablecloth width exceeds the width of fabric, piece panels together as follows:*

Tip

Select a medium- to heavy-weight cotton in a light color for tablecloth and coordinating quilting-weight cotton for the gift boxes.

• Draw a diagram to determine placement and width of panels (Figure 3).

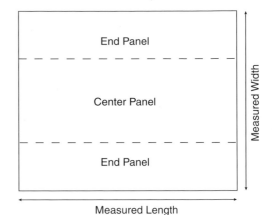

Figure 3

• Divide the cutting width by 3 to determine where the pieced seams will fall on the table. **Note:** *Ideally, seams should fall on top of the table and not within the lower 10 inches where the appliqués will be sewn.*

• Move position of the seams in either direction, allowing for a slightly wider or narrower center panel and keeping end panels of equal width.
• Add ½-inch seam allowance on inside seams and 2-inch hem allowance on outside edges to determine cutting width and length of each panel (Figure 4).

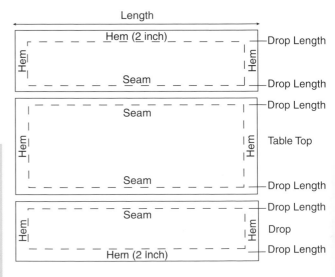

Figure 4

3. Draw tablecloth pattern with the dimensions determined in step 2 on pattern paper. Test layout of pattern paper tablecloth on your table to determine where seams will lie.

4. Determine the desired number and color of gift-box appliqués by placing fabric squares and paper patterns along edges of tabletop (Figure 5). **Note:** *Box appliqués will actually be placed lower on the cloth; avoid placing on corner fold.*

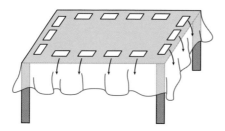

Figure 5

Cutting
From cotton tablecloth fabric:
• Use pattern(s) to cut panel(s).

From quilting fabric:
• Apply paper-backed fusible web to wrong side of each 11-inch square. Cut desired number of gift-box appliqués using square, rectangular and flat box appliqué patterns.

From medium-weight fusible interfacing:
• Trace gift-box pattern onto interfacing for each appliqué that is cut; cut out interfacing slightly larger than pattern.

Assembly
1. If using more than one panel, sew together and finish seams.

Tip

Read and follow package directions for the proper amount of steam, heat and pressure when using fusible interfacing and fusible web.

2. Turn under and press 1 inch on all edges. Turn raw edge in to meet crease and press a ½-inch double hem. Do not stitch at this time.

3. Position appliqués around perimeter of tablecloth, avoiding pressed-in hem and corners of cloth, and not exceeding 10 inches from outside edge. Fuse appliqués in place.

4. Fuse interfacing shapes on wrong side of tablecloth directly behind each appliqué.

5. Set sewing machine for satin stitch and attach appliqué foot. Satin-stitch edges of appliqués and detail lines.

6. Pin pompom-fringe trim to folded edge of hem and topstitch in place.

7. Tie each ribbon length in a bow and stitch or pin to tablecloth with safety pins. ￼

Sources: Fusible web and interfacing from Pellon; grosgrain ribbon and pompom fringe trim from Wrights.

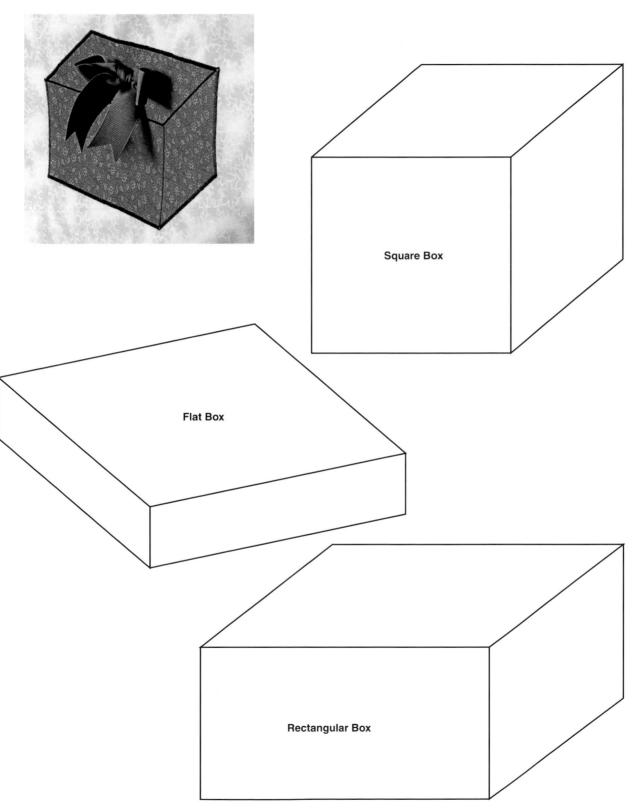

Square Box

Flat Box

Rectangular Box

A Pompom Party Table Topper Templates
Enlarge by 200%

All Zipped Up

Design by Janis Bullis

Add colorful protection to your patio table with an oilcloth cover that zips on around the umbrella pole. Use this classic no-ravel fabric to sew a super-quick project for outside entertaining.

Finished size
For table size, see chart on page 95

Materials
- Oilcloth or vinyl fabric for table cover (see steps 1–3 to determine required yardage)
- Pattern tracing cloth or paper
- Separating sport zipper 2–4 inches shorter than the tablecloth radius
- Optional: pattern weights or removable tape
- Narrow removable basting tape
- Teflon presser foot or tissue paper strips
- Yardstick
- T-square or right-angled ruler
- Paper and pencil
- Calculator
- Basic sewing supplies and equipment

Note: You may substitute woven fabric for oilcloth or vinyl if you prefer and eliminate the scallops. Cut the circle with the addition of a hem allowance for a double narrow hem all around. Use traditional seams and an exposed zipper application. Serge- or zigzag-finish the seam raw edges. Make a narrow double hem all around.

Determining Yardage
1. Measure the table diameter and make note. For cutting purposes later, divide by two to determine the table radius. ***Example:*** *A 42-inch-diameter table has a 21-inch radius.*

2. Determine the circumference (diameter x 3.14) and make note for determining the correct size for the scallop (see chart on page 95).

3. To determine the required yardage, select the table diameter and tablecloth size in the Tablecloth Yardage chart on page 95. As a general rule, for 54-inch-wide fabrics, you will need yardage equal in length to the table diameter. For narrower fabrics, you will need twice the diameter. Sizes allow for a 6–8-inch drop (including the scallops).

Note: You may need additional yardage to match printed motifs at the seam lines when joining fabric panels.

Cutting the Tablecloth Circle

1. On pattern tracing cloth, draw a square using the radius of the finished tablecloth. For example, for a 55-inch tablecloth, draw a 27½-inch square.

2. Draw a curve from one side of the square to the opposite side for the outer-edge cutting line. Draw a second curved line 3 inches inside the first to mark the placement for the inner points of the scallops. Draw a curved line 1½ inches from the corner to mark the cutting line for the umbrella pole opening. Add a ½-inch-wide seam allowance at one straight edge and mark (Figure 1).

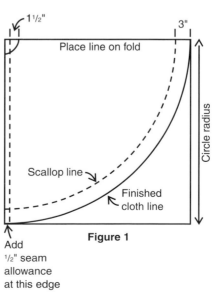

1½"

3"

Place line on fold

Circle radius

Scallop line

Finished cloth line

Add ½" seam allowance at this edge

Figure 1

3. Cut out the paper pattern along the curved lines for the pole and outer edge, and including the seam allowance added to one straight edge.

4. Fold the fabric with wrong sides facing and position the pattern piece. Use pattern weights to hold the pattern in place without pins, or try removable tape to anchor it to the oilcloth. Cut two pieces, making sure to flip the pattern to cut the second as a reverse image (Figure 2). Prior to cutting, match motifs if needed for printed or striped fabric. The motifs should match at the seam line—not at the cut edges.

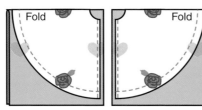

Figure 2

Assembly

1. With both halves of the tablecloth face up, trim the ½-inch-wide seam allowance from one seam edge above the pole opening. Trim ¾ inch from both straight edges below the pole opening for the zipper opening (Figure 3).

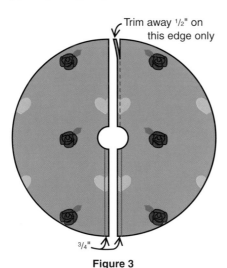

Trim away ¹/₂" on this edge only

³/₄"

Figure 3

2. Lap the cut edge over the remaining seam allowance, above the pole opening by ½ inch. Edge-stitch and topstitch, backstitching at the beginning and end of the seam (Figure 4).

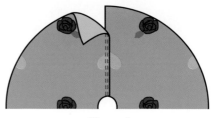

Figure 4

3. Apply basting tape to the wrong side of the zipper-opening edges. Remove the protective paper and position each cut edge ⅛ inch from the zipper teeth. Edge stitch.

4. To make a cutting pattern for the scallops, trim away, or turn under and press the ½-inch-wide seam allowance on the paper pattern for the tablecloth. Fold the pattern in half diagonally and press to crease. This crease marks the placement of the first scallop. To fit each tablecloth size, the size of the scallop will vary slightly. Refer to the Tablecloth Scallops chart (page 95) for the size you are making and make a half-circle paper pattern with the recommended scallop diameter. Mark the scallops along the edge of the pattern piece, centering the first one at the crease you made and ending with a half-scallop at each end (Figure 5). ***Note:*** *If the number doesn't quite fit, adjust a few of the inner scallops slightly. The differences won't be noticeable in the finished cloth.*

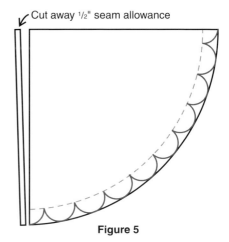

Cut away ¹/₂" seam allowance

Figure 5

5. Cut the scallops in the paper pattern. Position the pattern on the wrong side of the tablecloth circle and use a marking pen to trace around the scallop edges. Cut carefully along the marked lines. ❦

Fabric Yardage

Tablecloth Yardage

Table Diameter	Tablecloth Diameter	Fabric Width	
		36–45 inches	54 inches
34–38 inches	50 inches	3 yards	1½ yards
39–43 inches	55 inches	3¼ yards	1⅝ yards
44–48 inches	60 inches	3½ yards	1¾ yards
49–53 inches	65 inches	3¾ yards	1⅞ yards
54–58 inches	70 inches	4 yards	2 yards

Tablecloth Scallops

Table Diameter	Cloth Diameter per quarter	No. of Scallops Around ¼ Circumference	Scallop Diameter
34–38 inches	50 inches	8	4⅞ inches
39–43 inches	55 inches	8	5¼ inches
44–48 inches	60 inches	8	5⅜ inches
49–53 inches	65 inches	10	5⅛ inches
54–58 inches	70 inches	10	5½ inches

Knot-ical & Nice

Design by Janis Bullis

Wake up to nautical appeal with these simple place mats with grommets and cable cord.

Finished sizes
Place Mat: 12 x 18 inches
Optional Napkin: 16 x 16 inches

Materials for one place mat and napkin
• 44/45-inch-wide cotton fabric:
  ½ yard print for place mat center (and optional matching print napkin)
  ½ yard coordinating tone-on-tone print for borders and backing
• ½ yard 44-inch-wide lightweight fusible interfacing
• Grommet application tool
• 32 (¼-inch-diameter) silver grommets
• 2¼ yards ³⁄₁₆-inch-diameter cotton cable cord
• Basic sewing tools and equipment

Cutting
From the print for place mat center:
• Cut one 9 x 15-inch rectangle.
• Optional: Cut one 17-inch square for napkin.

From border/backing fabric:
• Cut one 13 x 19-inch rectangle for place mat backing.
• Cut two 3 x 14-inch strips for short borders.
• Cut two 3 x 20-inch strips for long borders.

From the fusible interfacing:
• Cut one 9 x 15-inch rectangle.
• Cut two each 3 x 14-inch and 3 x 20-inch strips for borders.

Assembly
Use ½-inch-wide seam allowances unless otherwise directed.

1. Fuse interfacing to the wrong side of the 9 x 15-inch center rectangle and the 3-inch-wide border strips.

2. On the wrong side of the center panel, mark the seam lines at all four corners. With right sides together and long cut edges even, center and pin one long band to one long edge of the center panel. With the center panel on top, stitch from seam-line to seam-line intersection. Begin and end with backstitching (Figure 1).

End stitching at seam intersections.

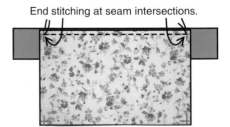

Figure 1

3. Add the remaining border strips in the same manner.

4. Trim the seams to ¼ inch wide and finger-press toward the place mat center.

5. To miter each corner, fold the mat diagonally with the long edges of the adjacent borders even. Draw a 45-degree-angle stitching line from the seam intersection to the outer edge; stitch on the line and trim the excess, leaving a ¼-inch-wide seam allowance (Figure 2).

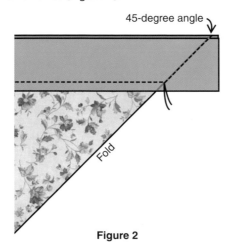

Figure 2

6. After mitering all four corners in this manner, press the border seam allowances toward the outer edges of the completed place mat front.

7. With right sides together, pin together place mat front and 13 x 19-inch rectangle for place mat backing; stitch ½ inch from raw edges, leaving a 6-inch-long opening in one long edge for turning. Backstitch at the beginning and end of the seam. Clip the corners, trim the seam allowances to ¼ inch and turn the place mat right side out; press, turning in the opening edges. Slipstitch the edges together.

8. Mark the grommet placements along all edges as shown in Figure 3. Apply the grommets through all layers following the package directions.

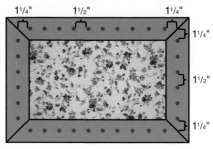

Figure 3

9. Lace cord through the grommets, tying a knot at each corner. To finish cord ends on the underside, cut the cord ends so they butt and whipstitch together. Wrap the ends with a scrap of fabric or ribbon, and glue in place with permanent fabric adhesive.

10. To finish the napkin square, turn under and press a narrow hem all around, and then topstitch or use your serger to finish the edges with a rolled edge.

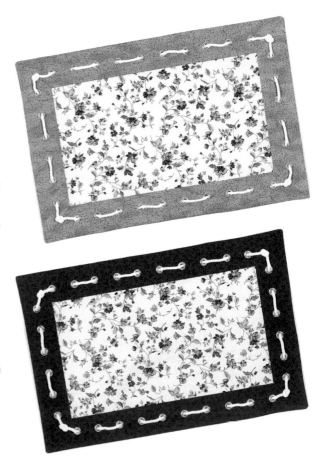

Let the Games Begin

Design by Janis Bullis

This is a sure bet. Make one large custom table mat to fit your card table perfectly, and your next card party will be a winner.

Finished size
34 x 34 inches

Materials
- 44/45-inch-wide medium-weight cotton fabric:
    - 2½ yards navy blue for center panel, binding and backing
    - 1 yard red for border
    - ⅜ yard white for circles
    - ¼ yard black icons
- ½ yard medium weight nonwoven fusible interfacing
- 1 yard paper-backed fusible web
- 34-inch-square low-loft quilt batting
- Basic sewing supplies and equipment

Cutting
From navy blue fabric for center panel, binding and backing:
- Cut one 43 x 43-inch square for backing.
- Cut one 23 x 23-inch square. Fold into quarters. Cut one center panel on the folded fabric using the pattern on page 101.
- Cut 3-inch strips across the bias to total 150 inches when pieced for binding.

From red fabric for border:
- Cut one 34 x 34-inch square. Fold into quarters.

Cut one border panel on the folded fabric using the pattern on page 101.

From white fabric for circles:
- Apply fusible web to wrong side of fabric. Using template provided on page 103, cut four 8-inch circles.

From black fabric for icons:
- Cut four 7-inch squares; apply fusible web to wrong sides. Using templates provided (page 103), cut one each diamond, heart, spade and club icon.
Note: To add more color to your card playing table mat, cut your heart and diamond appliques from red, and your spade and club appliques from black.

From fusible interfacing:
- Cut four 9-inch circles.

Assembly

Use ½-inch-wide seam allowance.

1. Beginning in center, mark five lines diagonally across center panel, spacing 4 inches apart. Mark in same manner in opposite direction so lines intersect, creating diamond patterns. Mark centers of straight and curved edges on both the border and center panel. Mark each outside corner of the border with a dot ½ inch from both edges (Figure 1).

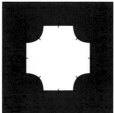

Figure 1

2. Stay-stitch inside corners of border ½ inch from edge; clip almost to stitching. Stay-stitch curved edges of center panel ½ inch from edge; clip almost to stitching in each corner and every ½ inch along curves (Figure 2).

Figure 2

3. With right sides of fabric together and raw edges even, pin inner edge of border to outer edge of center panel at center markings, then pin edges between centers. Stitch border to center panel; press seams.

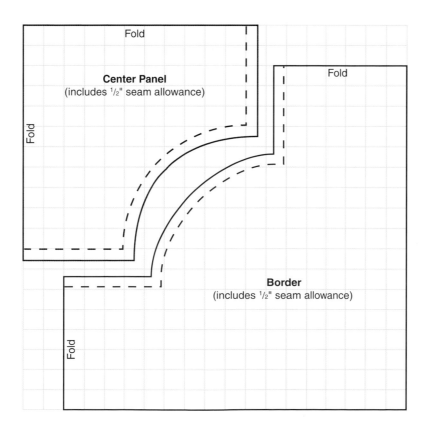

Let the Games Begin Patterns
1 square = 1"

4. On right side of mat, position and fuse an 8-inch circle at each corner of border 2 inches from center panel. Position and fuse an icon in the center of each circle. On wrong side of mat, position and fuse a 9-inch circle directly behind the 8-inch circles (Figure 3).

Figure 3

5. Using a very short, medium-width zigzag stitch and an appliqué foot, satin-stitch edges of circles and icons.

6. Sandwich batting between mat and backing; pin together, then baste ¼ inch along outer edge. Trim away quilt batting from seam allowance.

7. Straight stitch on marked lines on center panel, securing thread ends. Stitch ½ inch from seam line around perimeter of center panel.

8. Join bias strips; press under ⅝ inch on each edge. Bind edges of mat, stitching ¾ inch from outer edge and mitering corners at each dot (Figure 4).

Figure 4

9. Top-stitch mat ½ inch from binding.

Sources: Low-loft quilt batting from Fairfield Processing; fusible web and interfacing from Pellon.

Tip

Select your center and border fabrics in colors of equal value, then choose a light color value for the circle background to highlight playing-card icons.

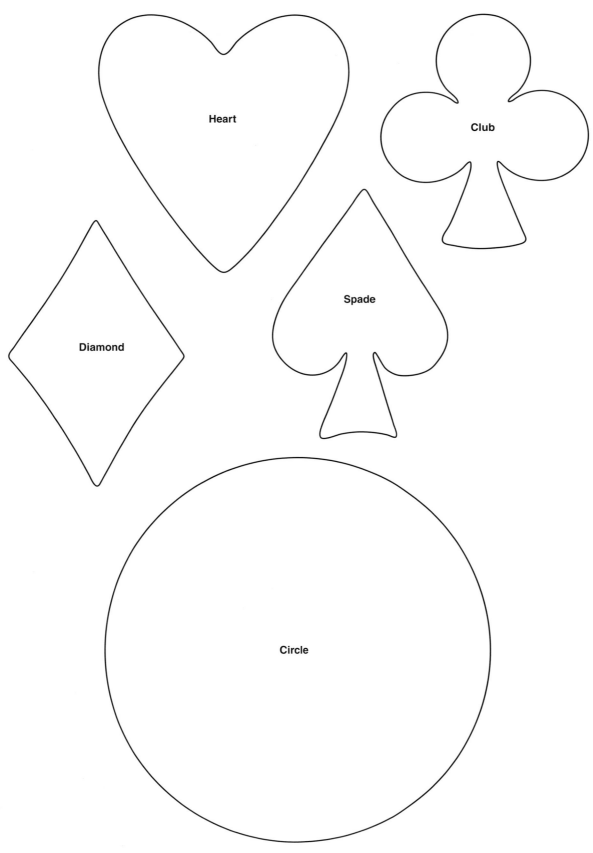

Heart

Club

Spade

Diamond

Circle

Let the Games Begin Templates
Enlarge 200%

Set a Summery Table

Designs by Linda Turner Griepentrog

Create a summery table setting sure to please—think of an afternoon tea or spending a relaxing Sunday morning on a shaded porch. Reversible napkins and place mats are great for mix-and-match settings. Silk flowers accent the no-sew, beribboned napkin rings.

Finished sizes
Tablecloth: 72 inches in diameter
Table Topper: 42 x 42 inches
Napkin: 20 x 20 inches
Napkin Ring: Approximately 1½ inches in diameter without flower
Place Mat: 14 x 18 inches

Materials
• 44/45-inch-wide fabric:
  4⅛ yards for tablecloth
  1¼ yards for table topper
  ⅝ yard each 4 coordinating fabrics for 2 reversible place mats and 2 reversible napkins
• ½ yard 45-inch-wide medium-weight fusible interfacing
• Picot-edge ribbon:
  3⅝ yards ⅜-inch-wide
  4⅛ yards ¾-inch-wide
• 3½ yards 1½-inch-wide wire-edged ribbon
• 1½-inch-diameter cardboard tube
• 2 silk flower stems with blossoms and leaves
• Optional: ¼- and ½-inch-wide double-stick fusible web
• Permanent fabric glue
• Texturized nylon thread and serger thread for place mat and napkin edging
• Basic sewing supplies and equipment

Cutting
From fabric for tablecloth:
• Cut two equal lengths. Cut one length in half along fold line to make two strips.

From fabric for table topper:
• Cut a 43-inch square.

From fabric for place mats and napkins:
• Cut four 15 x 19-inch rectangles for place mats, mixing and matching prints and colors.
• Cut four 21-inch squares for napkins, mixing and matching prints and colors.

From fusible interfacing:
• Cut two 15 x 19-inch rectangles for place mats.

Napkin & Place Mat Assembly

1. Press the napkin squares and place mat rectangles to remove wrinkles.

2. Lightly spray the wrong side of one napkin square with temporary spray adhesive and adhere it to the wrong side of its coordinating piece. Smooth in place, making sure the layers are bubble-free and the raw edges are aligned.

3. Adjust the serger for a rolled hem and use serger thread in the needle and texturized nylon in the loopers. Serge the napkin edges together, trimming ¼ inch from each edge and running the stitching off at each corner.

4. Following the manufacturer's directions, fuse interfacing to the wrong side of one fabric for each place mat. Fuse the interfacing to the lighter of the two colors for each place mat to prevent pattern show-through from the other print.

5. Lightly spray the wrong side of one place mat layer with temporary spray adhesive and adhere it to the wrong side of its coordinating piece. Finger-press in place to eliminate air bubbles.

6. Finish the edges of the place mats as directed in step 1 of Table Topper Assembly. Press completed napkins.

Table Topper Assembly

1. Serge-finish all edges of the table topper square. Turn under and press ½ inch on all four edges; stitch ¼ inch from folded edge.

2. Mark ribbon placement lines 3½ inches and 6¼ inches from the finished edges. Stitch the ribbon edges along the lines, mitering the corners as you sew (Figure 1). **Note:** *The wider ribbon should be closest to the table topper outer edge, and the ribbons should be 2 inches apart.*

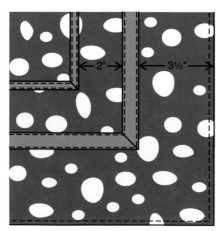

Figure 1

3. Press the completed topper.

Napkin Ring Assembly

1. From cardboard tube, cut two rings, each 1¼ inches wide. For each ring, cut a 38-inch length of wire-edged ribbon. Anchor one end of each ribbon to the inside of a cardboard ring with glue and allow to dry. Wind the ribbon in and out over the tube, arranging the ribbon at a slight angle as you overlap the edges and allowing the ribbon to pleat or gather a bit as you wrap it. Adjust the gathers or pleats as desired before gluing the ribbon end to the inside of the tube. Allow to dry.

2. For each napkin ring, remove a silk flower and one or more leaf groups from the floral stem. Glue the leaves to the underside of the silk flower; allow to dry.

3. From the remaining ribbon, cut two pieces each 15 inches long. Cut a V notch in the end of each length. Fold each ribbon in half crosswise. Glue folded end to the center of the napkin ring; allow to dry. Glue the silk flower on top of the folded ribbon.

4. Fold napkins so 1½ inches of the inside color shows above the outer color. Roll napkin up and tuck into the napkin ring as shown in photo.

Tablecloth Assembly

1. For the tablecloth, sew the half-width panels to opposite edges of the full-width panel. Use ⅜-inch-wide seam allowances and press the seams open (Figure 2).

Figure 2

Note: *If the selvages are smooth and flat, you can leave them on the fabric panels and join selvage edge to selvage edge for a ravel-free finish. If the selvages are tight and puckered, remove them before sewing the panels together, and then serge- or zigzag-finish the raw edges. If the fabric has a one-way design, match the design motifs at the seams so the pattern continues in one direction.*

2. Fold the fabric in half lengthwise and then crosswise with folds and edges even. Mark a 37-inch radius from the folded fabric point (Figure 3). Cut out the circle.

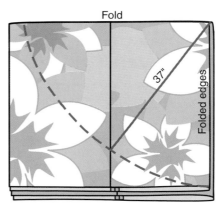

Figure 3

3. Serge-finish the cut edge; turn under and press a ½-inch-wide hem. Topstitch ¼ inch from the turned edge. Press the completed tablecloth.

Shoofly Butterfly Table Runner

Design by Carol Zentgraf

Create this pretty table runner with felted butterflies. Embellish each butterfly with wool roving, and your guests will never get enough of that wonderful stuff.

Finished size

Approximately 20 x 48 inches

Materials

- 36-inch-wide wool felt:
    - ½ yard each pistachio ice cream #0703, cotton candy #0905, English rose #0944, mulberry #0966, robin's egg #0580, periwinkle #0581 and blush #1601
- Needle-felt wool roving:
    - 1 skein each bluenote #0506, rain forest #0734, black #1000, keylime #0425, pink hibiscus #0961, green apple #0716, pink lemonade #0904 and powder blue #0518
- Felting needle tool and mat
- Individual felting needles
- Powdered artist pigments:
    - interference gold #674
    - duo red-blue #680
- Optional: No. 5 round paintbrush
- Permanent fabric adhesive

Instructions

Use patterns provided on page 110 and 111.

1. Cut four large butterflies from each felt color for a total of 28 large butterflies.

2. Cut two of each small butterfly from each felt color for a total of 28 small butterflies.

3. Arrange large butterflies on a flat surface in an area approximately 20 x 48 inches, overlapping. Fill in spaces with small butterflies, overlapping edges slightly. **Note:** *Cut more small butterflies as needed to fill space.*

4. Carefully lift up and glue overlapping edges. Let dry.

5. To felt, pull a small amount of needle-felt roving from the skein and arrange in desired shape on the felt. Place the felting mat under the area.

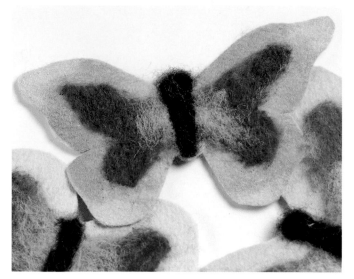

Use individual felting needle to shape the edges, poking the roving into the felt. Use the felting needle tool to pounce the surface of the roving into the felt until it is securely attached and shows on the wrong side of the felt. ***Note:*** *Apply main colors first; then add accent colors for shading or details.* Add a body to each butterfly with black roving.

6. Using the paintbrush or your finger, rub dry powdered pigments randomly on edges of butterfly wings to add iridescent accents. ☞

Sources: WoolFelt felt and WoolWisps roving from National Nonwovens; felting needle tool, mat and needles from Clover; Pearl Ex powdered pigments from Jacquard Products; Fabri-Tac permanent fabric adhesive from Beacon Adhesives.

Shoofly Butterfly Large Butterfly Pattern

Shoofly Butterfly Small Butterfly Patterns

Something to Crow About Penny Rug

Design by Pamela Cecil

This proud rooster is ready to crow, and you will be too when you see how easy it is to cut and stitch a penny rug for your table centerpiece.

Finished size
13½ x 17½ inches

Materials
• ⅝ yard black wool felt
• ¼ yard each wool felt in the following colors:
    crimson, off-white, yellow, bronze, pumpkin,
      copper, denim blue, moss green, gold
• Embroidery floss in the following colors:
    gold, yellow, light yellow, medium moss
      green, orange, burgundy, black,
      medium blue
• Paper-backed lightweight fusible web
• Pattern tracing cloth or tissue
• Chenille/candlewicking needle
• Scraps poster board or template plastic
• Basic sewing supplies and equipment

Instructions
1. Trace templates on pages 115–117 onto poster board or template plastic and cut out.

2. Using the dimensions given in Figure 1, draw a complete oval onto pattern tracing cloth or tissue.

Fold the black felt in half and pin the pattern in place. Cut out two ovals and set aside.

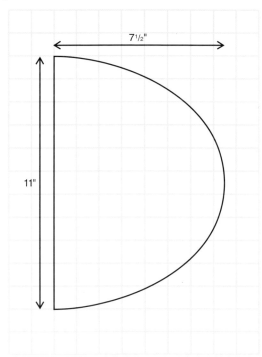

Figure 1
Oval Pattern
1 square = 1"

3. Trace around the large half-circle tab 16 times on the remaining doubled black felt. Cut out the sets of tabs and pin each set together.

4. Referring to the templates on pages 116 and 117, and the small half-circle tab template on page 115, trace the required number of each piece onto the paper side of the fusible web. Group pieces for each color and leave ¼ inch of space between the pieces. Cut out the pieces in groups and apply the fusible web to the appropriate-color felt. Cut out each felt piece and remove the paper backing.

5. Referring to the photo and the templates on pages 116 and 117, position the felt pieces in numerical order on one black oval. Fuse in place following the manufacturer's directions.

6. For the tabs, fuse the eight small yellow and eight small copper half-circle tabs to the upper black tab in each pair. Align the straight edges before fusing. Re-pin the tab sets together as you complete each one.

7. Using 3 strands of embroidery floss and referring to Figure 2, blanket-stitch around each piece of felt using the following colors:

• Black for rooster body.
• Gold for sunflower stems, moss green tail and wing feathers.
• Yellow for denim blue tail and wing feathers.
• Orange for sunflower buds, sunflower bloom, and rooster beak and feet.
• Burgundy for sunflower center and the six small circles.
• Light yellow for the rooster comb and wattle.
• Medium moss green for the bronze tail and wing feathers.
• Medium blue for the gold wing and tail feathers.

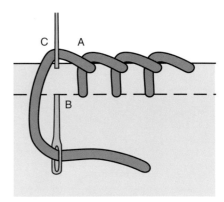

Figure 2

8. Using 3 strands of black floss, stitch a French knot through all layers in the center of the rooster's eye.

9. Use 3 strands of orange floss to blanket-stitch around the curved edge of the yellow half-circle tabs on the black tabs, stitching through the top black layer only in each tab pair. Use the burgundy floss to stitch the copper half-circle tabs in the same manner.

10. Use 3 strands of orange floss and make long cross-stitches to embroider the two large stars (Figure 3) above the rooster. Using 3 strands of gold floss, make the smaller star between the two larger ones.

Figure 3

11. Holding the tabs in matched pairs, use 3 strands of moss green floss to blanket-stitch around the outer curved edges of each pair of black tabs.

12. Arrange the tabs around the outer edge of the remaining black oval with the tab ends extending ¼ inch onto the oval edge. The side edges of the tabs may overlap each other slightly so that all tabs fit neatly around the oval. Pin in place and then baste, using 1 strand of black embroidery floss.

13. Position the appliquéd oval on top and pin in place. Use 3 strands of moss green floss to blanket-stitch around the edges of the upper oval, catching the tabs in the stitching. Repeat on the reverse side, catching the back of the tabs in the stitching. 🥄

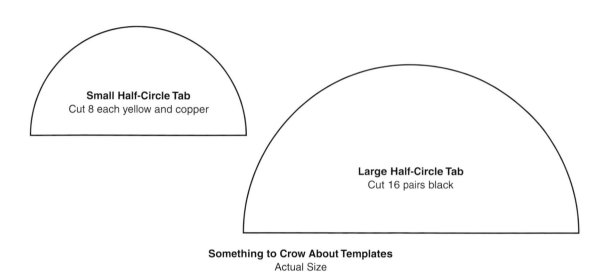

Small Half-Circle Tab
Cut 8 each yellow and copper

Large Half-Circle Tab
Cut 16 pairs black

Something to Crow About Templates
Actual Size

Perfect Points

To make neat stitches when turning corners or stitching around sharp points (feathers and comb tips), take a tiny extra stitch to tack down the blanket stitch at the tip. Bring the needle up from the back at the tip, catch the floss and insert the needle at the tip. Bring the needle back up at the tip and catch a few of the felt fibers to ensure that the tacking is secure (Figure 4). Continue with the blanket stitching.

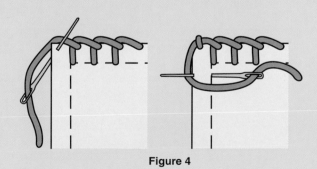

Figure 4

Cut 1 of each rooster piece

Something to Crow About Templates
Actual Size

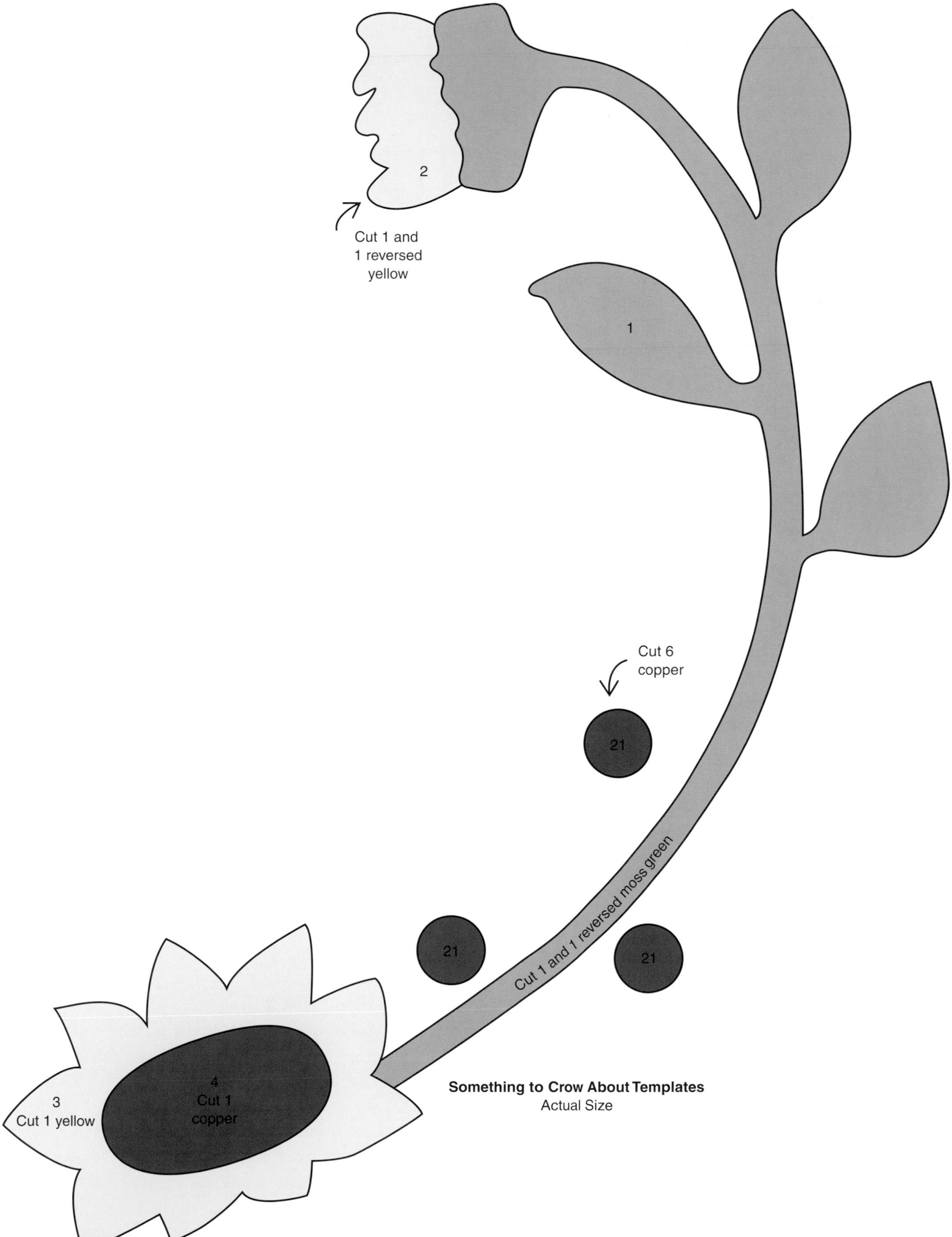

Cut 1 and
1 reversed
yellow

2

1

Cut 6
copper

21

Cut 1 and 1 reversed moss green

21

21

Something to Crow About Templates
Actual Size

3
Cut 1 yellow

4
Cut 1
copper

Sew Geometric Black & White Tablecloth

Design by Lorine Mason

Not just for wearables anymore, graphic border prints will dress your table with dramatic results!

Finished size

Approximately 93 inches in diameter

Materials

- 8½ yards 45-inch-wide floral border-print fabric
- ¼ yard fusible web
- Yardstick
- Basic sewing supplies and equipment

Pattern Preparation

1. Fold a 12-inch square of paper into 12 equal pie shapes. Cut along fold lines to remove one pie shape (Figure 1).

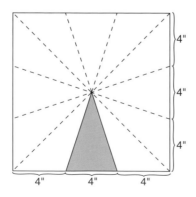

Figure 1

2. Place this pie shape on a new piece of paper with tip of shape centered on top edge of paper. Add ½ inch seam allowance to both sides, extending sides to bottom edge of paper (Figure 2). Cut out pattern (Figure 3).

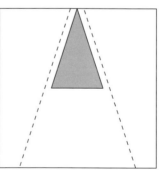

Figure 2   **Figure 3**

Cutting

- Lay fabric right side up on flat surface. Place pattern piece along top edge of fabric approximately 12 inches from left edge of fabric. Lay yardstick along left-hand edge of the pattern and use a fabric marker to mark a line to the bottom edge of the fabric, moving the yardstick along the same angle as you go. Repeat on

right-hand edge of pattern (Figure 4). Cut on marked lines (Figure 5). **Note:** *Bottom of triangle should measure 25 inches.* Use this fabric piece as the pattern to cut an additional 11 pieces, carefully placing the bottom edge of the pattern along the bottom edge of the border print.

Figure 4

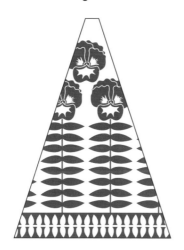

Figure 5

- Apply fusible web to wrong side of a section of fabric containing desirable floral designs for center appliqués. Cut out designs.
- Cut at least 120 (5-inch) squares of fabric for prairie-point trim. **Note:** *Seven folded squares, when sewn together, will create approximately ½ yard of trim.*

Assembly

Use ½-inch seam allowances throughout. Use an overcast stitch or serger to finish raw edges.

1. With wrong sides together, stitch the 12 fabric-triangle sections together.

2. Remove paper backing from floral appliqués. Fuse a single appliqué to wrong side of tablecloth center. Satin-stitch over edges of design.

3. On right side of tablecloth, fuse multiple appliqués to center, overlapping slightly. Satin-stitch over edges and add detail.

4. Fold each prairie-point square in half diagonally, wrong sides together; press. Fold again diagonally and press.

5. Place one triangle under the sewing machine needle with the fold to the back of the machine. Tuck the folded edge of a second triangle half-way into the first triangle and stitch across the raw edges, adding another triangle as you stitch. Continue to create length needed to sew around the bottom of the tablecloth.

6. Matching raw edges, pin prairie-point trim to the right side of the tablecloth; stitch. Clip into the seam line at each of the tablecloth seams. Press prairie-point trim down from the bottom edge of the tablecloth. 🖈

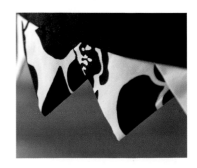

Accessories for the Fashionable Table

Great accessories enhance every fashion "plate," and a table is no different. Dress your table in style with these delightful bowls, bun warmers, napkins and more. And when the party is over, we've even designed beautiful storage covers to keep your fashion plate looking its best.

Fat-Quarter Gift Bag Centerpiece

Design by Cheryl Stranges

This stunning gift bag, made from cotton fat quarters, says "happy anniversary!" Make it quick, make it say what you want, and make it to give to your special guest at your next gala celebration.

Finished size
Approximately 12½ x 9 x 4 inches

Materials
• 2 fat quarters or ½ yard 45-inch-wide
  100 percent cotton fabric
• 1 yard fusible or moisture-activated
  cutaway stabilizer*
• ¼ yard firm-support nonfusible
  interfacing/stabilizer
• Seam sealant
• Universal size 14 serger needles
• Polyester serger threads:
  1 spool invisible
  2 cones white
  2 cones red
• Machine-embroidery thread:
  1 spool 40-weight rayon
  1 spool 40-weight metallic
  1 spool 60-weight white bobbin thread
• Mega machine-embroidery hoop
• Machine-embroidery designs:
  3-D Embroidery Decorative Font Breman UC,
    or embroidery design of your choice
  Isolde Staab #4125954-01 Sparklers
• Keyhole buttonhole cutter
• Small square ruler (2 x 2 inches or 2½ x 2½ inches)
• 1¼ yards ¼-inch-wide gold trim
  (practice amount included)
• 2 (10-inch) lengths ¼-inch gold cord
• Basic sewing supplies and equipment
*For a very stiff bag, double the amount of stabilizer
  and use 2 layers.

Note: When using fusible stabilizer, prewash fabric for proper application.

Cutting
Use rotary cutter and nonslip ruler.

From fusible stabilizer:
• Cut two 17 x 11½-inch rectangles.

From cotton fabric:

• With right sides together, cut two 17 x 11½-inch rectangles so grain runs with the 11½-inch length (Figure 1). Fuse stabilizer to wrong sides of cotton rectangles using a press cloth and cotton/steam setting on iron.

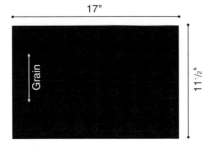

Figure 1

Option: Purchase nonfusible cutaway stabilizer and spray-baste stabilizer on wrong side of fabric following manufacturer's instructions. All outside edges must be spray-basted.

Using small square ruler, cut a 2-inch square from bottom corners of both rectangles (Figure 2).

Figure 2

Embroidery

1. Hoop one piece of stabilized cotton in mega machine-embroidery hoop. Using grid on embroidery screen, position letters with design (Figure 3).

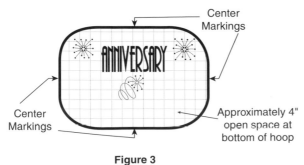

Center Markings

Center Markings

Approximately 4" open space at bottom of hoop

Figure 3

Note: When centering, keep in mind that at least 4 inches at bottom will be taken up with base allowance.

2. Mark four small lines to show positioning in hoop (Figure 4). Stitch design using 40-weight rayon thread for letters and metallic thread for sparkler design. When stitch-out is complete, remove from hoop and trim unwanted threads.

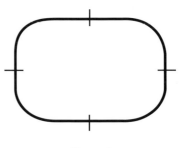

Figure 4

Serger Preparation

1. Thread serger for 4-thread serge: two red cone threads on needles and two white cone threads on upper and lower loopers.

Settings:
LN—normal
RN—normal
UL—normal
LL—normal
Stitch width—normal
Stitch length—2.5
Differential feed—1, if an option on your serger

Note: Always do a test run on fabric prepared the same way as project fabric and adjust tension accordingly.

2. With right sides together, serge side and bottom seams (Figure 5) or leave 1-inch open for wide trim application.

OR

1"

Figure 5

3. Pinch right sides of bottom cutout edges together to form ends for base, aligning bottom seam with side seams. **Note:** *Base of bag should measure 12½ x 4 inches.* Serge base end seams (Figure 6).

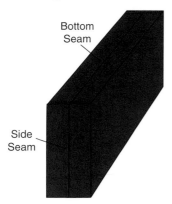

Bottom Seam

Side Seam

Figure 6

4. Turn bag right side out. Using press cloth, press out wrinkles. Finger-press four side edges and four bottom edges; iron (Figure 7). Push corners out using stiletto or point turner.

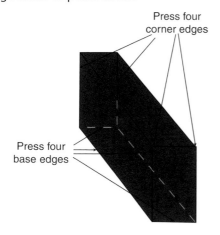

Press four corner edges

Press four base edges

Figure 7

3-Thread Serger Decorative Work

1. Convert the serger to 3-thread and free arm.

Settings:
LN—normal/red thread
RN—removed
UL—normal/invisible thread
LL—normal/white thread
Disengage cutting blade
Stitch width—N
Stitch length—3.0

Trim
Note: *Do a sample of the following step before working project.*

2. Using the pearl foot, lay trim inside hollowed area of foot and pull it through this area toward the back about 2 inches past the needle. Start the serge at the side of the gift bag, but not on a seam. Serge the trim to the upper edge of the gift bag, overlapping the end portion about ½ inch.

Keyhole Buttonholes
1. Mark keyhole buttonhole locations approximately 7 inches from each side seam and ¾ inch from upper edge (Figure 8). Stitch buttonholes using recommended buttonhole foot.

Figure 8

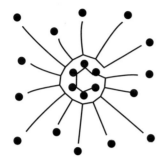

2. Apply a drop of seam sealant on each buttonhole; let dry completely.

3. Using keyhole buttonhole cutter and mat, cut out keyhole center areas.

Finishing

1. Insert ends of cord through buttonholes, knotting on inside. Apply a drop of seam sealant to each knot and let dry.

2. Cut a 12 x 4-inch piece of firm-support non-fusible interfacing; trim to fit inside base of bag and insert.

Note: *If desired, cover interfacing with fabric before placing in bottom of bag.*

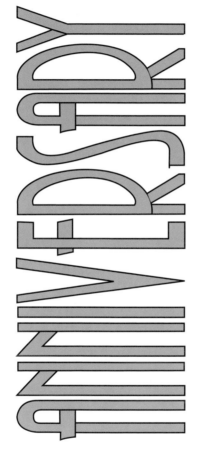

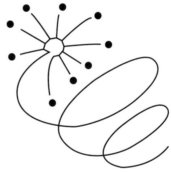

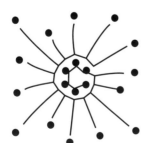

Embroidery Pattern
Enlarge 125%

Yo-Yo Christmas Tree Table Topper

Design by Linda Turner Griepentrog

Add yuletide cheer to your holiday table with a simple-to-make yo-yo tree. The circular sections can be gathered by hand or machine, and a bit of stuffing keeps them puffy. For a truly inspired sewing touch, use a wooden spool as the base.

Christmas Tree

Finished size
14 inches tall

Materials
- 10 scraps assorted green print fabric
- 16 inches ¼-inch-diameter wooden dowel
- 1½ x 2⅛-inch wooden spool
- 2 (1⅞-inch) star buttons
- Polyester fiberfill
- Red and green pearl cotton or other large thread
- Fabric glue
- Metallic acrylic paint:
    green
    gold
- Small paintbrush
- Compass or circle templates
- Basic sewing supplies and equipment

Cutting

From green print fabric:

• Using a compass or circle templates, cut 10 circles in 1-inch increments from 12 inches to 3 inches in diameter.

• Cut a very small slit (less than ¼ inch) in the center of each circle.

Assembly

1. Using metallic acrylic paints, paint wooden dowel with green; paint wooden spool with gold. Let dry.

2. Wind red pearl cotton snugly around wooden spool using a drop of fabric glue at the beginning and end to anchor.

3. Glue at least ½ inch of wooden dowel in hole in spool; let dry.

4. To make yo-yos, sew a basting stitch ⅛ inch from the outside edge of each circle; pull bobbin-thread ends to gather, lightly stuffing each circle with fiberfill before tying off thread ends.

5. With gathered sides of yo-yos facing up, insert dowel through center slits of nine yo-yos, from larger to smaller.

6. Leaving room at the top of the dowel for the star buttons, arrange yo-yos to fill the space. Secure positions with glue if needed.

7. Slide tenth yo-yo over top of dowel, gathered side down.

8. Tie green pearl cotton through holes in star buttons. Glue buttons to top of dowel.

Wine Charms

Design by Kristine M. Frye

Materials

• Beading hoops or ring-sized memory wire coil
• Assorted beads
• Charms
• Needle-nose pliers or chain-nose pliers

Instructions

Notes: *Match colors and charms to the occasion you are celebrating. If using memory wire instead of beading hoops, cut one coil of wire and bend one end into a small loop before stringing beads.*

1. String beads to fill half of one wire loop.

2. Add charm, then string the same number of beads as on first half of loop.

3. Using pliers, bend a hook in open wire end so it fits into loop on opposite end.

Gather Up!

To make it easier to tell which thread is the bobbin thread, use different colors of green for top and bobbin side.

Places, Please

Design by Pauline Richards

Place cards add a finishing touch to a well-set table. Choose holiday or seasonal fabric to complement linen or china and make them all the same—or personalize them for each guest with different fabrics and trims.

Finished sizes

3 x 4½ or 4 x 4½ (before folding)

Materials

- Assorted 5½ x 10-inch fabric scraps,
  1 for each place card
- Heavyweight double-sided fusible craft stabilizer
- ¼-inch-wide fusible web tape
- Fusible metallic ribbon
- Ribbons to coordinate with fabrics
- 1 spool ⅛-inch-wide gold wire-edge ribbon
- Assorted embellishments: charms, pins, buttons
- Teflon press cloth
- Teflon sole plate
- Tear-away stabilizer
- White or cream card stock
- Pinking shears (or decorative blades for
  the rotary cutter)
- Optional: fabric prepared for ink-jet printing
- Dritz Ezy-hem measuring tool (for photo
  corner card)
- Craft glue
- Basic sewing supplies and equipment

Note: You may substitute a layer of heavyweight stabilizer and two layers of fusible web (one for each side of the stabilizer) and adapt the directions as needed to utilize these layers if the double-sided fusible stabilizer is not available.

Basic Place Card Assembly

Refer to the Emily place card for the directions that follow.

1. For each place card, cut two 2 x 3-inch rectangles from the double-sided fusible stabilizer. From the desired fabric, cut one 4 x 5-inch fabric rectangle.

2. Arrange the stabilizer rectangles side by side on the wrong side of the fabric with ⅛ inch of space between the inner long edges (Figure 1).

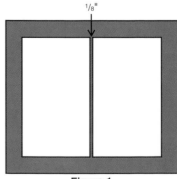

Figure 1

3. Turn in opposite raw edges onto the exposed fusible stabilizer and use the tip of your iron to fuse in place. ***Note:*** *Use the Teflon press cloth to protect your iron.* Repeat with the remaining opposite raw edges (Figure 2), trimming excess fabric in the corners for a smooth, neat finish.

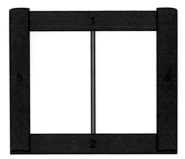

Figure 2

4. To form card holders, position coordinating ribbon pieces (Figure 3) and wrap 1 inch of ribbon to the wrong side. Trim. Apply glue to ribbon ends, tuck underneath, finger-press into place and allow to dry.

Back of card

Fold

Front of card

Figure 3

5. Position fusible web tape on the four edges on the card wrong side with the tape at least ⅛ inch from the outer edges (Figure 4).

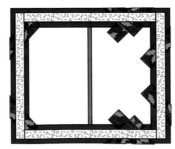

Figure 4

6. Use pinking shears or a decorative rotary blade to cut a fabric rectangle slightly smaller than the card measurement. Center fabric over the fusible tape, and holding fabric it in place, fold the card in half to shape the holder. Trim edges if needed. Open card and fuse inner fabric in place. Refold the card and press to shape.

7. Cut a 1½ x 2¾-inch piece of paper or card stock and write the guest's name on the card. ***Option:*** *Use the computer to print a name in your favorite font size, shape and color on fabric treated for ink-jet printing. Leave the release paper on the back of the fabric and cut to size.* Tuck corners of name card under ribbons and secure to front of holder with a small piece of double-sided tape.

Note: *To create a simpler card, follow the basic directions above, but apply ribbons to only two corners before securing the inner fabric, folding and fusing. Embellish with a simple bow.*

Get It Cornered

Add fabric photo corners embellished with iron-on ribbon trim to hold the name card.

1. For each place card, cut three 2 x 3-inch rectangles from the double-sided fusible stabilizer. From desired fabric, cut one 4 x 5-inch rectangle, one 3 x 4½-inch rectangle and one 1 x 10-inch strip for a set of four photo corners.

2. Make a place card using two pieces of stabilizer and the larger fabric rectangle as directed in steps 2 and 3 for the basic place card. Cover the remaining piece of stabilizer with the smaller fabric rectangle for the place card front.

3. Use pinking shears or a decorative rotary blade to cut a fabric rectangle slightly smaller than the measurement of the basic card. Refer to steps 5 and 6 for the basic place card to cover the underside of the card and press to shape the card.

4. To make the photo corners, turn under and press ¼ inch along one long edge of the 1 x 10-inch strip. Attach the Teflon sole plate to your iron. Position the fusible trim ¹⁄₁₆ inch from the folded edge and press into place, using only the protected point of the iron (Figure 5).

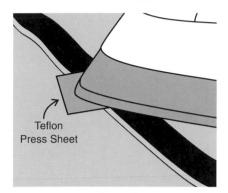

Figure 5

5. Cut four 2½-inch pieces from the strip. Place one strip right side down and center the corner of the Dritz Ezy-hem measuring tool as shown with both turned edges aligned with the ⅞-inch mark (Figure 6).

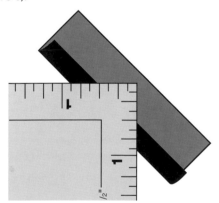

Figure 6

6. Fold the fabric around the ruler corner and press to set (Figure 7). Repeat with the remaining strips to create four photo corners.

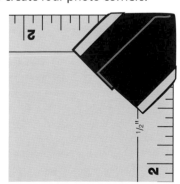

Figure 7

7. Slip the photo corners over the corners of the card front and use a little craft glue to secure them to the underside.

8. Apply a light coat of craft glue to the back of the card front; position glue side down on the front of the basic card and smooth in place. Allow to dry.

9. Create the name card and tuck in place under the photo corners.

Embroidered Cards

Use your embroidery machine to create beautiful fabric cards. The finished size of an embroidered card will depend on the font and lettering size you use and the border you add.

1. Create the desired name and border in embroidery editing software and transfer to your embroidery unit.

2. Hoop the fabric and embroider the design in the desired colors, using stabilizer to support the fabric and prevent puckering.

3. Use the embroidered fabric to create the card front and follow the directions for the basic card on pages 130 and 132. Use the Teflon press cloth to protect the fabric and embroidery when fusing the card layers in place.

4. Trim the edges with pinking shears or a decorative rotary-cutting blade, and embellish with a pin or button at one corner. 🖈

Perfect Corner Napkin

Design by Julie Johnson

You will find this technique so fast and easy, you'll be creating beautiful matching napkins for all your table wear.

Finished size

16 x 16 inches

Materials for four napkins

- 1 yard 44/45-inch-wide cotton or linen fabric
- Serger
- Basic sewing supplies and equipment

Instructions

1. Cut four 16½ x 16½-inch squares from fabric (or desired size). **Note:** *Finished size will be ½ inch smaller than the cut size.*

2. Set serger for a rolled edge.

3. Roll-edge one complete side of fabric square. At corner, carefully sew one stitch past the raw edge of the napkin.

4. Raise the presser foot and gently pull on the needle thread below the tension to loosen the thread for turn.

5. Turn napkin fabric and reposition corner so that the needle of the serger connects with the previously rolled edge. Lower pressure foot and gently pull on the needle thread above the tension to retighten thread.

6. Roll-edge next two edges using same procedure at corners.

7. On fourth side of napkin, roll-edge off the fourth corner. Apply seam sealant and clip threads. 🖈

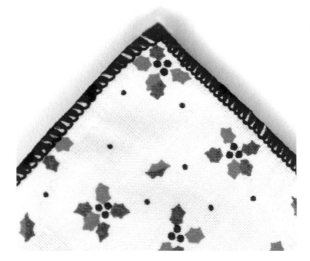

The Standing-Fan Napkin Fold

Elegant and decorative, this is a classic napkin-folding technique. As usual, an iron helps but is not necessary.

1. Fold the napkin in half and orient the open end toward you (Figure 1).

Figure 1

2. Fold the napkin like an accordion, starting at either narrow end. Leave one end with 2–3 inches of unfolded napkin to support the standing fan (Figure 2).

3. Fold the napkin in half with the accordion folds on the outside (Figure 3).

4. Grasp the unfolded corners where they meet on the open end and fold them in diagonally, tucking them under the accordion folds (Figure 4).

5. Open it and stand it up (Figure 5)—a beautiful fan for a beautiful dinner!

Figure 3

Figure 4

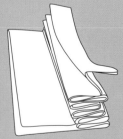

Figure 2

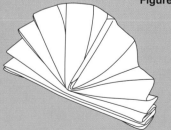

Figure 5

Skirted Serving Side Table

Design by Lorine Mason

Table space at a premium? Try this elegant solution at your next dinner party. No need to overcrowd—simply set extra dishes to the side within easy reach on a portable table.

Finished size
25½ inches long

Materials
- 2¾ yards 48-inch-wide fabric
- 4 yards each ⅝- and 1-inch-wide grosgrain ribbon
- 4 (1¼-inch) buttons
- 14 x 19-inch wooden folding table
- Staple gun
- Basic sewing supplies and equipment

Cutting
- Cut three pieces of fabric each 32 x 48 inches. Trim away selvage edges.

Assembly
Use ½-inch seam allowances throughout. Use an overcast stitch or serger to finish raw edges.

1. With right sides together, stitch together short ends of fabric sections to make one long piece.

2. Turn under 3 inches along one long edge; press. Turn under 3 inches again; press and pin to hold. Stitch along top folded edge.

3. Center 1-inch-wide grosgrain ribbon over stitched hemline, stitching along both edges of ribbon. Stitch ⅝-inch-wide ribbon over center of 1-inch-wide ribbon.

4. Turn under 3 inches on left edge of fabric; press. Turn under 3 inches again; press and pin to hold. Using a decorative stitch, stitch through all layers of fabric close to inside folded edge; stitch again close to outer folded edge. ***Note:*** *Stitch just to the top of the grosgrain ribbon, repeat on right-hand side of skirt, until completely topstitched.* Using a decorative stitch, stitch through center of grosgrain ribbon across the length of the skirt.

5. Overlap the left-hand front hemmed edge of the skirt over the top of the right-hand front edge and pin to hold. Fold table skirt into quarters and mark each of the points with a pin along the top edge.

Note: *Center front point will fall in middle of the overlapped front hem.*

6. Turn portable table upside down. Measure and mark a line ¾ inch from the outside edges around the underside of the table. Also mark the center points on each edge.

7. Place the right side of the table skirt's center front edge ¼ inch inside the pencil line. Staple through fabric into the bottom of the table on the pencil line. Staple the center back and center sides in the same manner.

8. Pinch fabric between each of the stapled centers, pulling it out toward the table corner. Mark the center point with a pin. Measure ¾ inch from either side of the pin mark and mark with

pins. Remove center pin. Fold the 1½ inches into a mitered fold and staple to corner of table. Repeat for remaining three corners.

9. Fold remaining fabric between corners and centers into inverted box pleats and staple in place. Turn table over and check skirt for correct fullness. Make adjustments if necessary. Invert table once more; staple fabric in place around the table circumference as close to the outside of the table edge as possible.

10. Sew buttons to the center front of the table skirt, stitching through all layers of fabric to close the opening.

Daisy's Fruit Tea

The sweet, fruity flavor is perfect for an afternoon in the shade.

1 (12-ounce) can frozen orange-pineapple juice concentrate
1 (6-ounce) can frozen lemonade concentrate
4 cups water
2 family-size tea bags
1¼ cups sugar
Orange for garnish

Thaw juice and lemonade. Boil water and remove from heat. Add tea bags and steep for 15 minutes. Remove tea bags and stir in sugar until dissolved. Add juice and lemonade and mix well. Pour into gallon-size pitcher and add enough water to fill. Stir. Chill and serve over ice with a thin slice of orange to garnish. Makes 1 gallon.

Holiday Coasters

Design by Marta Alto

These little wine-glass slipcovers are perfect for holiday entertaining any time of the year. Make a simple wine-glass charm for a sure-to-be-appreciated hostess gift.

Finished size
4 x 4 inches

Materials for one coaster
- Scraps 2 coordinating prints dupioni silk for coaster top
- Scrap cotton fabric for coaster base
- Woven or weft-insertion fusible interfacing
- Optional: serger
- Basic sewing supplies and equipment

Note: *Silk dupioni coasters add an elegant touch to holiday decorating schemes. If you prewash the silk before making coasters, you will be able to launder them as needed.*

Cutting
From scraps of dupioni silk fabric for coaster top:
- Cut one 4½ x 4½-inch square from each print.

From cotton fabric for coaster base:
- Cut one 4½ x 4½-inch square.

From interfacing:
- Cut one 4½ x 4½-inch square.

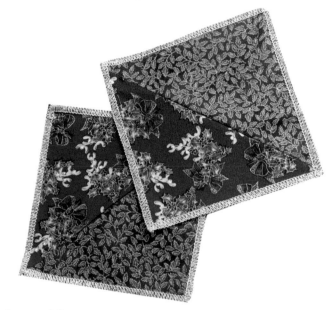

Assembly
Use ¼-inch seam allowance.

1. Fuse interfacing to the wrong side of coaster base square.

2. On the wrong side of one coaster top square, draw stitching lines as shown in Figure 1 on page 140. Place both coaster top squares right sides together and stitch on the lines, leaving a 3-inch opening in the center. Begin and end each section of stitching with backstitching.

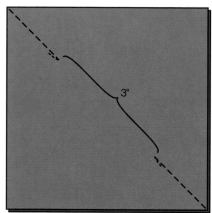

Figure 1

3. Press so the wrong sides of each triangle are together and there is an opening in the center (Figure 2).

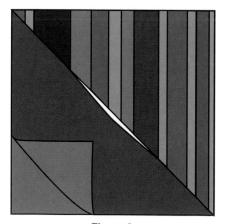

Figure 2

4. Stitch the top-square unit to the right side of the base square, beginning and ending the stitching on one side, not at a corner.

Note: *For smoothly turned corners that don't "poke" out, sew a slightly deeper seam (it will look bowed) on each side of the corner. A few stitches before the corner, stop and shorten the stitch length to 1.5mm and take one or two stitches across the corner (Figure 3).*

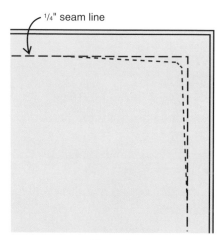

¹/₄" seam line

Figure 3

5. Clip the corners to remove excess fabric. Turn right side out and press. 🖊

Tip

To add decorative edges to your coasters, place the top square on the interfacing side of the base square and serge with a wide, closely spaced stitch and decorative thread.

Sushi Time Place Mat

Design by Linda Turner Griepentrog

Enjoy sushi and sauce with this fun twin-circular design to give each element its place.

Finished size
19 x 12½ inches

Materials
- ⅜ yard 45-inch-wide oriental-print cotton fabric
- 1½ yards contrasting double-fold bias tape
- Lightweight batting
- 2 inches ¼-inch-wide black elastic
- Chinese coin and bead
- Temporary spray adhesive
- Basic sewing supplies and equipment

Cutting
From oriental-print fabric:
- Cut two 13 x 20-inch rectangles.

From batting:
- Cut one 13 x 20-inch rectangle.

Assembly
1. Using temporary spray adhesive, adhere the wrong side of each fabric rectangle to each side of batting rectangle.

2. Enlarge place mat pattern 200 percent. Trace pattern onto top fabric layer. Machine-stitch on traced line; trim close to stitching.

3. Bind raw edge with double-fold bias tape.

4. Make a small elastic loop; stitch ends together through the mat at location indicated on pattern. Sew Chinese coin and bead over ends of elastic loop.

Hot Tip!

If you plan to serve hot food on the mat, use a batting with a thin metallic layer embedded in it, like Insul-Bright from The Warm Co.

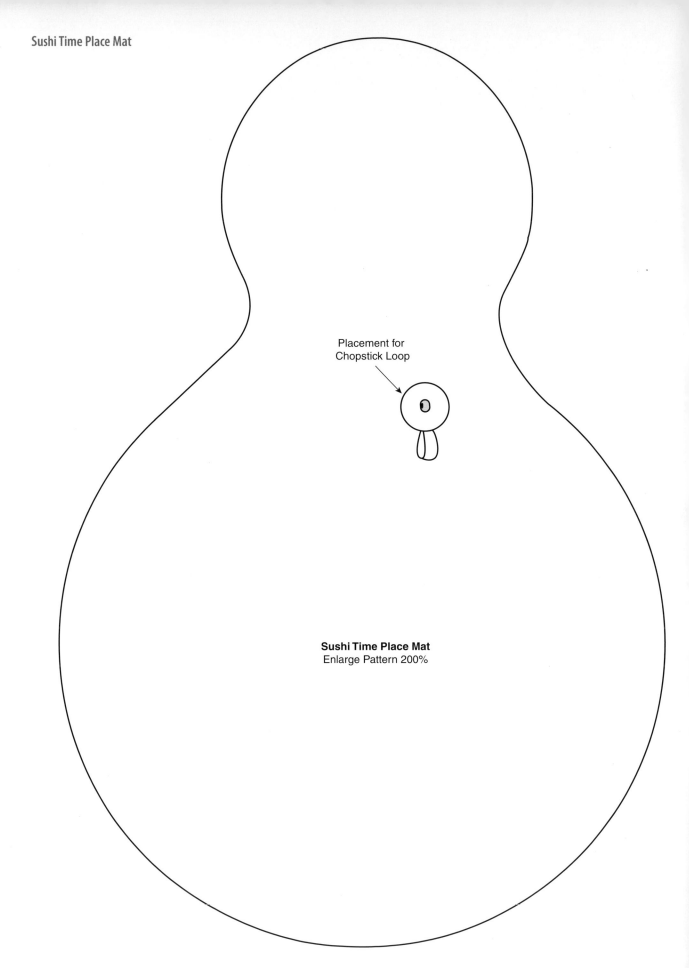

Placement for
Chopstick Loop

Sushi Time Place Mat
Enlarge Pattern 200%

Havana Breezes

Design by Margot Potter

Create a pretty napkin ring for any occasion
with simple beading techniques.

Materials
- Mother-of-pearl spine beads
- 2 (8-inch) lengths .039-inch-diameter elastic
  beading cord

Assembly
1. Slide spine beads on one length of elastic
beading cord for approximately 5 inches. Double-
knot ends together; trim excess cord. Repeat for
remaining length of elastic beading cord. ♀

A Tisket, a Tasket, Make a Bread Basket

Design by Pauline Richards

Low-sew projects are always fun and this Batik bread basket is a winner. Make a few for gift-giving or some for different holidays. Storage isn't a problem because the basket will store flat.

Finished size
Approximately 10 x 2½ inches

Materials
• ½ yard Batik fabric
• 15 x 15-inch sheet double-sided fusible, heavy craft interfacing
• ⅜-inch-wide water-soluble double-sided adhesive tape
• 6 Chinese ball buttons with loops
• Teflon press cloth
• Basic sewing supplies and equipment

Instructions
1. Using patterns provided (page 148), cut one base and six sides from interfacing.

2. Place Batik fabric right side down on ironing surface. Place interfacing pieces on wrong side of fabric as shown in Figure 1, allowing ⅛ inch between sides and base. Cover with Teflon press cloth and press pieces to fabric.

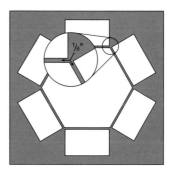

Figure 1

3. Trim around pieces as shown in Figure 2, allowing ½ inch seam allowance on outer edge.

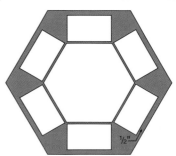

Figure 2

4. Using cut-out hexagon shape as a pattern, cut another piece from fabric for basket lining.

5. On basket, fold ½-inch seam allowance to inside and press with iron (Figure 3).

6. Adhere fusible adhesive tape to seam allowance following manufacturer's instructions (Figure 4).

Note: *Tape should be approximately ⅛ inch from folded edge.*

Figure 3

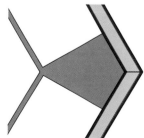

Figure 4

7. Position Chinese ball buttons and loops around edge of basket as shown in Figure 5 and press onto adhesive tape.

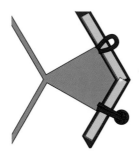

Figure 5

8. Carefully position basket lining inside basket, matching edges. Fold ½-inch seam allowance to inside and finger-press in place so edges of lining are even with basket edges.

9. Thoroughly press to secure basket lining to basket. Straight-stitch around basket ⅛ inch from edge.

10. With fingernail, define stitching lines between each side piece and between sides and bottom;

mark lines with chalk (Figure 6). Straight-stitch on marked lines.

Figure 6

11. Fold sides of basket up, and slip loops over buttons to secure.

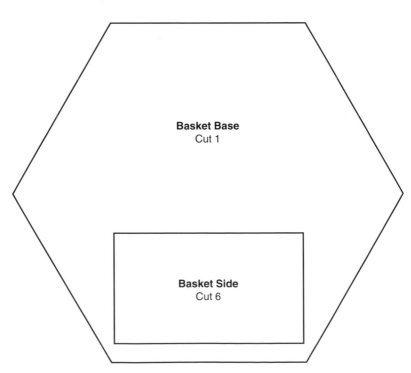

Basket Base
Cut 1

Basket Side
Cut 6

A Tisket, a Tasket, Make a Bread Basket Templates
Enlarge 200%

Tranquility

Design by Laurie D'Ambrosio

Soothing shades of blue and green beads combine in this set to use during relaxing evenings on the deck!

Materials
• Flat-handled flatware
• Green seed beads
• 26-gauge green wire
• Round-nose pliers
• Wire nippers
• Metal adhesive
• Tape

Note: *When beading, attach tape to wire ends to secure beads.*

Instructions

1. Wash flatware and dry. Cut a 24-inch piece of 26-gauge wire. Attach tape to one end and string on seed beads until two inches of wire are left. Tape wire end.

2. Beginning near base of flatware handle, apply 2¼ inches of adhesive to front and back. Beginning on the back, wrap the beaded wire around the handle, pressing beads into the adhesive. Remove tape from ends and glue ends to handle on reverse side. When adhesive is dry, trim excess wire.

Perfect Dinner Napkins

Design by Cheryl Stranges

Make professionally finished napkins with the rolled edge on your serger. You'll never purchase fabric napkins again.

Finished size
14½ x 14½ inches

Memory Wire Napkin Rings

Design by Kristine M. Frye

Materials
• Memory wire, bracelet size or smaller
• Assorted bugle beads
• Needle-nose pliers or round-nose jewelry pliers
• Memory wire shears (preferred) or wire cutters

Instructions
Note: Memory wire comes coiled in a specific size and does not change shape easily. Consider the size of your napkin when purchasing the wire coil.

1. Count 4–5 coils of memory wire and cut.

2. With pliers, bend one end into a small loop to keep beads from slipping off. String beads onto wire.

3. Bend another small loop at end of wire to secure beads.

Materials for four napkins
• ½ yard 60-inch-wide cotton, linen or synthetic fabric
• Size 80 Schmetz universal or size 80 microtex needle
• Lightweight tear-away stabilizer
• Serger
• Basic sewing supplies and equipment

Machine Settings
Note: Instructions are given for 2-thread rolled edge. A 2-thread narrow, or 3-thread narrow or rolled edge could also be used.
Appropriate fabric type
Stitch length 1.0 R-setting
Differential feed: 1.0 Rt-N 3 LL=6
Stitch finger engaged

Instructions
1. Cut four 15 x 15-inch squares from fabric (or desired size). *Note: Finished size will be ½ inch smaller.*

2. Cut tear-away stabilizer into 1-inch-wide strips. Place one strip under fabric edge and serge edge, leaving a thread chain at ends. Trim away fabric edge and stabilizer ¼ inch. Tear away stabilizer. Repeat on remaining edges.

3. Apply a drop of seam sealant at each corner; let dry. Trim thread ends. ✐

Serving Soft-Box

Design by Lynn Weglarz

Sew this deceptively simple fabric box to hold your pretty paper napkins. Your guests will be impressed with your cooking and creativity. Cleanup is easy: simply store flat when finished.

Finished size
12 inches in diameter

Materials
• ⅓ yard each 2 coordinating fabrics
• ⅓ yard lightweight batting
• 2 yards ⅝-inch-wide grosgrain ribbon
• 1-inch bias-tape maker
• Optional: basting spray
• Basic sewing supplies and equipment

Cutting
• Cut one 12-inch-diameter circle from each fabric and from batting.

• On the bias, cut 2-inch-wide strips from one fabric to make a 42-inch length of bias tape.

• Cut eight 9-inch lengths of ribbon.

Assembly
Note: Refer to Serve-It-Hot Roll Warmer on page 154 for bias tape instructions.

1. Spray-baste or pin-baste batting circle between wrong sides of fabric circles. Measure and mark a line along each side of the layered circle 2 inches from the outer edge (Figure 1).

2. Measure and mark a point 2 inches to the right and 2 inches to the left of each corner of marked square; pin the end of one grosgrain ribbon at each marked point (Figure 2). Baste ribbon ends in place.

3. Stitch bias tape around outside edge of circle, making sure to encase ribbon ends (Figure 3). Fold ends of bias under at joining.

4. Trim ribbon ends at an angle. To use, tie each pair of ribbons into a bow to create a box. ❦

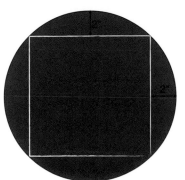

Figure 1

Figure 2

Figure 3

Serve-It-Hot Roll Warmer

Design by Lynn Weglarz

So easy to sew, so pretty to see, sew this reversible roll warmer to coordinate with every holiday table setting! Simply slip the roll warmer into your pretty basket and serve.

Finished size
16 inches in diameter

Sewing Tips

• Use a zigzag or serpentine stitch rather than a straight stitch when sewing on bias tape. These stitches will move with the bias tape, allowing the bottom edge of the tape to be caught in the sewing.

• If you wish to line the roll warmer, follow the same instructions, but cut four circles of fabric. Baste two circles together; apply bias tape.

• Instead of bias tape, circles can be serged around with a balanced stitch for a very fast and easy hostess gift!

Materials
• ½ yard each 2 coordinating fabrics
• 1-inch bias-tape maker
• Basic sewing supplies and equipment

Cutting
• Cut one 16-inch-diameter circle from each fabric.

• On the bias, cut 2-inch-wide strips from each fabric to make two 55-inch lengths of bias tape.

Bias Tape
1. From each fabric, position two strips at right angles to each other with right sides together and raw edges even (Figure 1). Using a ¼-inch seam, stitch across raw edge. Press seam open and trim triangles. Repeat as needed to make 55 inches long.

Figure 1

2. Insert one end of strip through bias tape maker (Figure 2). Pull strip through several inches and press. Continue pulling strip through, pressing as you go.

Figure 3

Figure 2

3. Bring folded edges of strip together, extending one side slightly so it is wider than the other; press (Figure 3).

Assembly

1. For each circle, position a bias strip from contrasting fabric around edge of circle with wide side of strip on wrong side of circle. Fold ends under at joining. Stitch using a zigzag stitch.

2. Layer circles together and fold into eight equal sections; press to mark. Unfold and stitch on pressed marks to create eight triangular compartments for rolls.

The Lily Goblet Fold

The Lily Goblet Fold (as shown on page 151) has an elegant look that is made easier with a slightly starched or stiff napkin.

1. Fold the napkin into quarters (Figure 1).

3. Fold the napkin in half as shown (Figure 3).

Figure 3

4. Tuck the napkin into the glass of your choice (Figure 4).

Figure 4

5. Using your fingers, gently pull apart the loose corners sticking up so they are evenly distributed. If your flaps don't want to stay where you put them, then ironing a little starch into the napkin will help (Figure 5).

Figure 1

2. Accordion-fold the entire napkin from corner to corner, keeping the open ends at the top (Figure 2).

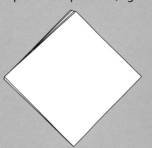

Figure 2

Figure 5

Twisted Basket & Quilted Table Topper

Designs by Susan Breier

What says unique better than this pretty round bowl resting on top of a matching quilted table topper.

Finished size

Basket: 7-inch-diameter at base, 11½-inch-diameter at top, 4½ inches tall

Table Topper: 21½ inches square

Materials

- 65 feet ³⁄₁₆-inch flexible clothesline with no hard center core
- 8 different-color fat quarters of cotton fabric for basket strips (3 colors are also used for borders and binding of table topper)
- ⅔ yard 45-inch-wide cotton fabric for front center panel and four cornerstones of table topper and strips for basket
- ⅞ yard 45-inch-wide coordinating piece of cotton fabric for table topper backing
- 25 x 25-inch square low-loft batting
- 20 (¾-inch) flat buttons
- New 80 or 90 universal machine needles
- Variety of hand-sewing needles
- 50 (1-inch) brass safety pins or 50 straight pins
- 2 acid-free glue sticks
- Masking tape or colored tape
- Needle-nose pliers
- Bamboo stick or stiletto
- Single-stitch foot and throat plate for table topper
- Zigzag foot or open appliqué foot and zigzag throat plate for basket
- Acrylic extension table or equivalent (to extend level sewing surface)
- Basic sewing supplies and equipment

Cutting

Use rotary cutter, mat and ruler.

From fabric for center panel and cornerstones:

- Cut one 16 x 16-inch square for center panel.
- Cut four 3½-inch squares for cornerstones.

From fabric for backing:

- Cut one 25 x 25-inch square for backing.

From fat quarters for borders, binding and basket:

- Cut four 1½ x 18-inch strips from each of three different-color prints for table topper borders.

• Cut 2¼-inch-wide strips on the bias to total 52 inches when joined for binding. **Note:** *Use same color as selected for border strip next to center panel.*
• After other pieces have been cut, begin rotary-cutting ½- to ¾-inch-wide strips for the basket. **Note:** *Cut only a few strips at a time to conserve fabric and prevent fraying from handling.*

Table Topper Assembly

Use a ¼-inch-wide seam allowance unless otherwise stated.

1. Place the 12 border strips in four groups of three each. Straight-stitch together each group of border strips. Press seams toward what will be the outer edge.

2. Trim two of the four assembled borders to 16 inches. Straight-stitch these pieces to two opposite sides of the 16-inch center panel (Figure 1). Press seams.

Figure 1

3. Trim remaining assembled borders to 16½ inches long. Sew a cornerstone to each end of each remaining assembled borders. Press seams. Straight-stitch assembled pieces to remaining sides of center panel unit (Figure 2). Press seams. Trim edges even.

Figure 2

4. With wrong side up, tape backing piece tautly on a flat, even work surface. Center the 25 x 25-inch square of batting over backing, then center the pieced top over the batting with right side up. Using safety pins or straight pins, pin together layers, beginning in center and working outward.

5. Remove tape. Beginning at the outer edge of one cornerstone, straight-stitch across the cornerstone diagonally to the opposite corner. Stitch diagonally across the cornerstone between opposite corners (Figure 3).

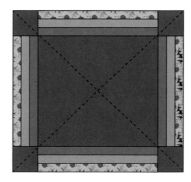

Figure 3

6. Make a 1-inch-wide paper guide to help stitch a total of seven straight lines centered diagonally across the center panel in both directions (Figure 4).

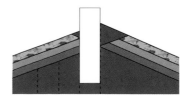

Figure 4

7. Stitch in the ditch at border and cornerstone seams, working diagonal lines on each cornerstone as you come to it.

8. Machine-baste ⅛ inch around outer edge of assembled center panel. Trim off excess batting and backing.

9. Bind edges with 2¼-inch-wide bias strips using a ⅝-inch-wide seam allowance and trimming seam to ⅜ inch.

10. Hand-stitch a button in the center of each cornerstone.

Basket Assembly

Use either zigzag foot or an open appliqué foot and zigzag bed.

1. Apply glue to 1 inch of both the wrong side of the fabric strip and the end of the clothesline. Wrap approximately 4 inches of line with fabric; pin in place to hold. Beginning at the end, straight-stitch a basting line for 2 inches (Figure 5). Remove from the machine and cut threads. Continue wrapping fabric around line, occasionally using a dab of glue.

Figure 5

Sewing Tips

A Must: Clean and oil machine before beginning. Insert a new needle.

Preparing Fabric: Always wash, machine dry and iron fabric before beginning project.

Hint: When wrapping, glue and pin at the beginning and the end of each strip to help hold it in place until the area has been sewn. Don't wrap more than a yard of line at a time. Always sew whatever you have glued. Dried glue may make your stitches irregular.

Keeping Track of the Tail: The tail is the wrapped line ready to be sewn. Keep the tail moving through the area that forms the arch or very center of your machine bed. Check this often as it is common to reverse the coil.

Consistent Stitches: Using zigzag attachments, make several wrapped sample lines to test which setting for zigzag is best. The stitches should touch adjacent lines evenly without entering the very center of the lines. Ideally the tops of the zigzags are ⅛ inch apart. Write the correct setting on tape and place it on the front of your machine as a reminder.

Fixing Mistakes: Occasionally, after wrapping and stitching, a portion of the line may show through. Use a permanent marker to color in a very small area. If you need to cover a larger area, cut a scrap of the same-color fabric, and glue and stitch it in place. Check for areas where stitches are off. Go back to that area and restitch. No one will ever know!

Joining Lines: It is easy to join lines together. Glue and overlap the unwrapped lines by ½ inch. Hold the area together. Wind an 18-inch piece of thread tightly around the joined area. Finger-press to decrease bulk and wrap tightly with fabric; zigzag while glue is wet.

2. Tightly coil wrapped line so it is about the size of a 50-cent piece. ***Note:*** *Use the machine bed to help maintain that shape.* Straight-stitch an "X" over the coil for easier zigzagging later (Figure 6). Remove from machine and cut threads.

Figure 6

3. Using a predetermined stitch setting (see **Consistent Stitches** tip in sidebar) zigzag edges of line together, starting at beginning of the coil (Figure 7). ***Notes:*** *Use the needle-down option to hold the line under the presser foot and free both hands. You will need to reposition the coil often because of stitching in a small area. A bamboo stick or stiletto will help twirl the coil under the needle.* Continue wrapping and zigzagging until the coiled base is 1⅞ inches in diameter.

Figure 7

4. Choose a different-color fabric strip. Overlap the end of the previous fabric and pin together. Continue wrapping and stitching as before.

5. Add new colors of staggered lengths of fabric to achieve a patchwork affect. When base reaches a diameter of 7 inches, prepare to begin shaping the sides. Place a piece of tape on the coil to the left of the needle to mark where to change hand positions (Figure 8).

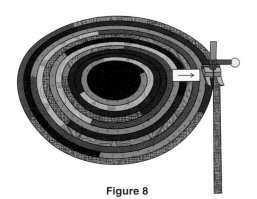

Figure 8

6. At the tape marker, with the needle down, lift the base halfway between the machine bed and the flat side of the needle arm (Figure 9). Zigzag one row until you again meet the marker. Stop with the needle down.

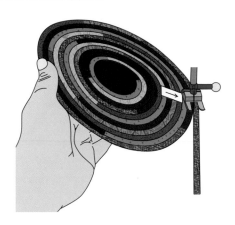

Figure 9

7. Change hand position so base touches the side of the needle arm (Figure 10). Continue stitching until the side measures 2 inches at the marker.

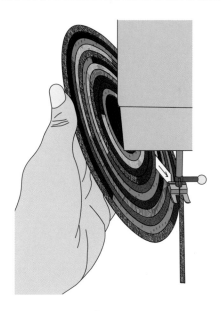

Figure 10

8. At this point, allow the side of the basket to fall onto the extension table as you sew. The top of the basket will widen and create V-shaped sides. Continue in this position until the side measures 4 inches at the marker (Figure 11 on page 162).

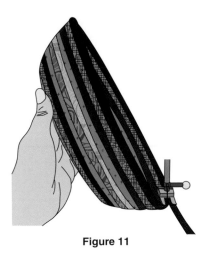

Figure 11

to just-wrapped fabric. Cut off remaining fabric and zigzag this area to finish the rim of the basket.

Note: *Use a bamboo stick or stiletto to guide this end of line tightly to the adjacent row. If end is bumpy, push straight pins into the rim and leave in place until glue dries.*

11. To help prevent the top from fraying and to strengthen the project, secure the top edge by zigzagging around it once on the fabric and one more time just off the rim.

12. Embellish the top edge of the basket with 16 (¾-inch) buttons sewn evenly spaced around the top three rows. **Note:** *Needle-nose pliers will help pull the needle through the thickness.* Cut off fraying threads. ♀

9. Wrap and zigzag three continuous rows using a focal color.

10. To finish off the end, apply glue to the fabric only and wrap line more firmly so the end tapers

Glazed Figs With Soft Cheese Sauce

The figs served with the Blue Cheese Cream sauce make a delicious appetizer. Served with the sweetened cream sauce, they become a unique dessert.

½ cup orange juice
¼ cup balsamic vinegar
¼ cup sugar
1 teaspoon orange zest
½ teaspoon vanilla
16 fresh figs or 20 dried figs
Blue Cheese Cream
Sweet Cheese Cream

Combine the orange juice, balsamic vinegar, sugar and orange zest in a small saucepan. Boil over high heat, stirring to dissolve the sugar. Reduce heat to medium and simmer for 5 minutes. Take off heat and stir in vanilla. If using dried figs, stir into warm glaze and heat through. If using fresh figs, cut them in half and cover with glaze; broil cut side up until lightly caramelized. Serve with cheese cream of choice.

Blue Cheese Cream

2 cups soft mascarpone, cream or goat cheese
½ cup heavy cream
¼ cup Gorgonzola cheese

Sweet Cheese Cream

2 cups soft mascarpone, cream or goat cheese
½ cup heavy cream
2 tablespoons confectioner's sugar
¼ teaspoon vanilla

For either cheese cream, whip soft cheese with an electric mixer until smooth. Continue whipping and slowly add cream in a steady stream. Add sugar and vanilla or the Gorgonzola respectively and continue whipping until fairly smooth.

Chalk It Up! Cheese Board

Design by Linda Turner Griepentrog

Cheese-and-wine–tasting parties are great fun.
Encourage party guests to sample cheese types on this
pretty chalkboard fabric tray to avoid flavor surprises!

Finished size
23 x 19 inches

Materials
• 1½ yards 47-inch-wide chalkboard fabric
• ⅞ yard 45-inch-wide food-print cotton fabric
• Lightweight cotton batting
• Temporary spray adhesive
• Chalk
• Basic sewing supplies and equipment

*Notes: Before use, cure chalkboard fabric by rubbing
the entire surface with chalk; clean with a damp
sponge or felt eraser and repeat.*

*Chalkboard fabric can be sewn with a regular sewing
machine needle (size 80/12) and all-purpose sewing
thread. Chalkboard fabric is not machine washable.*

*Do not cut food directly on the chalkboard fabric.
Use a small plate, cutting board or tile to protect
chalkboard fabric.*

Cutting
From chalkboard fabric:
• Cut a 16½ x 12½-inch rectangle for mat center.

Not Into Cheese Tasting?

This cute fabric-framed chalkboard is great to
hang on the kitchen wall to keep track of the
grocery shopping list or recipe of the day.

From cotton fabric:
• Cut two 12½ x 4-inch and two 23½ x 4-inch strips for border; cut one 23½ x 19½-inch rectangle for backing.

From lightweight batting:
· Cut one 23½ x 19½-inch rectangle.

Assembly
Use ¼-inch-wide seam allowances throughout.

1. Sew border pieces to chalkboard fabric, beginning with 12½-inch edges (Figure 1).

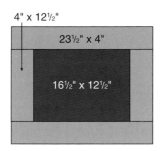

4" x 12½"

23½" x 4"

16½" x 12½"

Figure 1

Note: Carefully press seam allowances toward border, keeping iron away from chalkboard fabric to avoid melting.

2. Lightly spray underside of framed mat with temporary adhesive and smooth it flat over batting. Baste outer edges in place; trim batting to mat size.

3. With right sides together, stitch mat and backing edges together, leaving a 6-inch opening for turning. Turn right side out and hand-stitch opening closed. ◗

Zippy Hot Pepper Spread

This taste-bud-tingling appetizer is embarrassingly simple, yet so delicious. Serve it with an assortment of crackers.

1 (8-ounce) jar medium-hot green-pepper jelly or jalapeño jelly
1 (8-ounce) package cream cheese, softened

Spread jelly over cream cheese block. Serves 8 to 10.

The Silver Solution Silverware Holder

Design by Lynn Weglarz

This set of silverware holders made from Silvercloth will help prevent your silver from tarnishing. It's a unique cloth which has been embedded with thousands of particles of silver that capture the tarnish-causing gases before they reach the silver article stored inside, thereby ending the need to polish!

Finished size
31 x 13½ inches

Materials for five holders
- 2⅔ yards 58-inch-wide brown Silvercloth
- ⅛ yard 45-inch-wide cream satin
- ¼ yard lightweight paper-backed fusible web
- 1⅞ yards cream satin cord
- ¼ yard tear-away stabilizer
- Decorative thread for appliqué
- Machine-embroidery needle
- Basic sewing supplies and equipment

Cutting
From Silvercloth:
- Cut a 31½ x 22-inch piece for each holder.

From satin:
- Apply fusible web to wrong side of satin. Trace appliqué patterns (page 168) on paper side of fusible web and cut out on traced lines.

Assembly
1. Stitch all four edges of Silvercloth ¼ inch from raw edges. Turn under edge on stitched line. Using decorative thread and machine-embroidery needle, stitch close to fold using a 3.0–3.5mm stitch length. At corners, miter-press edges as shown in Figure 1. Trim edges close to stitched line.

Figure 1

2. Fold up 8 inches on one long edge; press. Following previous row of stitching, topstitch sides to form a pocket; topstitch ¼ inch from bottom folded edge.

3. Stitch 12 vertical rows 1¾ inches apart and parallel to sides, making 12 pocket divisions for each utensil as shown in Figure 2.

Figure 2

4. On outside of holder, position and fuse satin appliqué 1 inch from bottom fold and 1¼ inches from side edge. Turn holder over; position a piece of stabilizer opposite appliqué as shown in Figure 3.

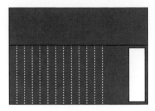

Figure 3

5. Satin-stitch around edges of appliqué through all layers of fabric. Remove stabilizer.

6. Cut a 12-inch length of cord; tie a knot on each end. On inside of holder, bar-tack one end of cord to appliqué end of holder close to side edge.

7. To use, insert one silver piece into each pocket division. Fold excess fabric over silverware and roll up holder; wrap cord around and tuck in knot to secure.

Silvercloth Care

Even though Silvercloth is cotton, washing will destroy its ability to prevent tarnish. To remove dust or other particles from the Silvercloth, simply use a piece of tape or lint roller to clean fabric.

Over time the Silvercloth will discolor and fade; this discoloration is the fabric itself tarnishing.

Never use rubber bands or other rubber elastic products on Silvercloth.

The Silvercloth will continue to prevent tarnish as long as the fabric remains intact.

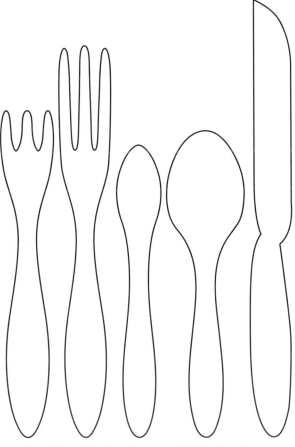

The Silver Solution Silverware Holder Templates
Enlarge by 200%

Store & Serve Plate Caddies

Designs by Carol Zentgraf

Store your dishes in style with protective quilted cases that serve double duty as attractive caddies for a dinner party or picnic. When used for storage, the lid attaches securely with hook-and-loop tape. To use as serving caddies, simply remove the lid and fold the upper edge of the case down.

Finished sizes
Dinner Plate Caddy: 12 x 5 inches
Salad Plate Caddy: 10 x 5 inches

Materials for each caddy
• ⅔ yard 45-inch-wide double-face quilted cotton fabric
• 4½ yards coordinating double-fold bias tape
• 1⅛ yards ¾-inch-wide sew-on hook-and-loop tape
• Permanent fabric adhesive
• Basic sewing supplies and equipment

Cutting for dinner plate caddy
From double-face quilted fabric:
• Cut two 12-inch-diameter circles for top and bottom.
• Cut one 39 x 6-inch strip for bottom side.
• Cut one 39 x 2-inch strip for top side.

Cutting for salad plate caddy
From double-face quilted fabric:
• Cut two 10-inch-diameter circles for top and bottom.
• Cut one 32 x 6-inch strip for bottom side.
• Cut one 32 x 2-inch strip for top side.

Assembly

Serge seams, or stitch using a scant ¼-inch-wide seam allowance and finish seams with a zigzag stitch.

1. Stitch short edges of bottom side piece together with inner sides together. Cover seam with bias tape (Figure 1). Repeat for top side piece.

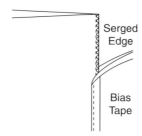

Serged
Edge

Bias
Tape

Figure 1

2. Fold each side piece in fourths and mark folds with pins. Fold top and bottom pieces in fourths and mark in same manner (Figure 2).

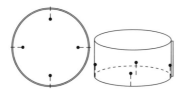

Figure 2

3. Open pieces and pin top and top side, inner sides together, matching quarter marks and easing sides to fit. Pin bottom and bottom side together in same manner. Stitch together and bind seams.

4. Finish raw edges of top and bottom sides; bind with bias tape.

5. On outside of bottom side, use chalk wheel to mark a line 1¾ inches from upper edge of side.

6. Pin the loop side of hook-and-loop tape around sides, aligning upper edge of tape with chalk line. Stitch both edges of tape to side using thread to match inner fabric.

7. Using permanent fabric adhesive, glue hook side of hook-and-loop tape to inside lower edge of top side; let dry thoroughly.

8. To use for storage, stack plates in caddy up to 5 inches high. Fold upper edge of side over plates and attach lid using hook-and-loop tape. To use for serving, remove the lid and fold over the top edge of bottom side to conceal the hook-and-loop tape.

Table Setting

1. Folded napkin
2. Plate
3. Soup bowl
4. Bread and butter plate with butter knife
5. Water glass
6. White wine glass
7. Red wine glass
8. Salad fork
9. Fish fork
10. Dinner fork
11. Service knife
12. Fish knife
13. Soup spoon
14. Dessert spoon and cake fork

Dining Table Leaf Covers

Design by Sheila Zent

After holiday or vacation visits are over, it's time to take the leaves out of the dining table and get the dining room back to normal. Before you stow them in the closet or under your bed, whip up storage covers in no time. Flannel-backed vinyl keeps the surfaces protected and free from scratches and dust.

Finished size
Size varies

Materials
- Flannel-backed vinyl: enough to cut 2 pattern shapes for each table leaf
- ¾-inch-wide hook-and-loop tape: 1 length equal to first width measurement for each table leaf cover
- Banner paper or nonwoven/nonfusible interfacing for pattern
- Basic sewing supplies and equipment

Pattern Preparation
1. Measure width, length and depth of one leaf (Figure 1).

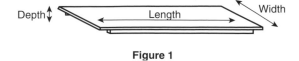

Figure 1

2. To calculate the cut width (A), add the width and the depth measurements, and then add an additional 2 inches for seam allowance and ease.

3. To calculate the cut length (B), add the length and the depth, and then add an additional 4 inches for seam allowance, ease and overlap.

4. Divide the depth measurement by 2 for the bottom measurement (C).

5. On pattern paper, draw a rectangle the calculated cut width (A) and cut length (B). Draw a square dimension of C in each lower corner (Figure 2).

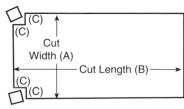

Figure 2

Special Thanks

Please join us in thanking the talented designers listed below for dressing our tables so fashionably.

Marto Alto
Falling Leaves Luncheon Set, 41
Holiday Coasters, 139

Pam Archer
Beading Sensation, 68
Fall Foliage, 52
Finely Feathered, 56

Susan Breier
Twisted Basket & Quilted Table Topper, 157

Brother International Corporation
Patriotic Party Set, 32

Janis Bullis
A Halloween Harvest, 48
A Pompom Party Table Topper, 87
All Zipped Up, 92
Knot-ical & Nice, 96
Let the Games Begin, 99
Sewing Seashells by the Seashore, 36

Pamela Cecil
Something to Crow About Penny Rug, 112

Michele Crawfield
Love Is in the Stars!, 18

Laurie D'Ambrosio
Tranquility, 149

Lucy A. Fazely and Michael L. Burns
Bali Tablecloth, 75

Kristine M. Frye
Wine Charms, 129
Memory Wire Napkin Rings, 150

Linda Turner Griepentrog
Chalk It Up! Cheese Board, 163
Make It Merry Mats, 64
Set a Summery Table, 104
Sushi Time Place Mat, 142
Yo-Yo Christmas Tree Table Topper, 127

Julie Johnson
Perfect Corner Napkin, 134

Pam Lindquist
Go Fly a Kite!, 22

Lorine Mason
Sew Geometric Black & White Tablecloth, 118
Skirted Serving Side Table, 136

Margot Potter
Havana Breezes, 145

Pauline Richards
A Tisket, A Tasket, Make a Bread Basket, 146
Places, Please, 130

Cheryl Stranges
Fat-Quarter Gift Bag Centerpiece, 122
Perfect Dinner Napkins, 150

Carolyn Vagts
Bee-Dazzled Summer, 44
Bunny in Style, 28
Easy-to-Grow Poinsettia, 59
Sweet on You, 13

Viking Sewing Machine Co.
Shadow-Stitched Table Runner, 10

Lynn Weglarz
Serve-It-Hot Roll Warmer, 154
Serving Soft-Box, 152
Summer Bright Tablecloth, 85
The Silver Solution Silverware Holder, 166

Shelia Zent
Dining Table Leaf Covers, 172

Carol Zentgraf
Coming Up Flowers Table Runner, 72
Cut It Out: A Tablecloth Makeover, 78
Organza Table Runner & Chair Topper, 6
Ribbons Galore, 81
Shoofly Butterfly Table Runner, 108
Store & Serve Plate Caddies, 169